The 30-Day Wellness Alchemist Detox

Awaken Your Inner Healer

TANYA MARKUL & ANDRÉA BALT
WWW.REBELLEWELLNESS.COM

The 30-Day Wellness Alchemist Detox:
Awaken Your Inner Healer

DISCLAIMER. The information provided in this book is designed to provide helpful information on the subjects discussed. This book is not meant to be used, nor should it be used, to diagnose or treat any medical condition. For diagnosis or treatment of any medical problem, consult your physician. The publisher and authors are not responsible for any specific health or allergy needs that may require medical supervision and are not liable for any damages or negative consequences from any treatment, action, application or preparation, to any person reading or following the information in this book.

Table of Contents

Signs you are ready for a detox.

The following is not a comprehensive list, but a compilation of some of the most common symptoms that you may be ready for a healthy change...

Physical symptoms:
- Frequent fatigue, sickness/colds and/or tension headaches.
- Irregular bowel movements, bloated stomach, constipation.
- Dark eye circles, frequent skin break-out, coated tongue, frequent sinus infections, bad breath.
- Tight or sore muscles, back pain, muscle aches and cramps.
- Frequent physical discomfort, inability to relax.

Emotional symptoms:
- Nervousness, unmotivated anger.
- Feeling stuck, imprisoned and helpless.
- Confusion, lack of clarity.
- Mood swings, constant irritation, negative attitude.
- Inability to forgive and let go.
- Inability to live in the moment (too much focus on the past and/or future).
- Stress and tension.
- Impatience with yourself and others.
- Constantly giving up and starting over.
- Persistent self-destructive thoughts.
- Inability to commit to a healthy regime and to stick to it.
- Feeling overly critical, nit-picky or judgmental.
- Obsession with food, especially unhealthy food.

Optimal health is not a condition or a personal quality but a matter of daily choice and commitment.

We are a process in constant creation and change — and so is our health. Our body is our gateway into the world and it deserves and demands the best care we can offer it. Developing this conversation with our body takes time and a deep understanding of our own individual needs. Why have this conversation? Because good health allows and invites abundance on every level of our lives so that we can live with awareness, sensitivity, honesty and beauty beyond our imagination.

Our bodies can get caught in a toxic cycle of bad habits, especially when it comes to food. This cycle doesn't only affect our physical body, but also our mental state, our mood and thereby the overall quality of our lives.

If you want to change your life and rid yourself of the physical and emotional symptoms tormenting you, you have to be willing to start somewhere — that somewhere is right now, right here as you are, and your diet is that starting point.

Introduction.

Welcome to the first thirty days of your lifetime detox. All you need to get started is the sincere desire to deepen the exploration of yourself, the courage to look, feel and inquire within, and the trust in that you already have everything you need (mentally and physically) to create a more intimate, nourishing and healthy relationship with food, yourself and life.

This is not your typical detox. It does not include consecutive days of fasting, an all-raw food diet, skipping meals, fads or special drinks. You won't have to purchase any special herbs, supplements or system-shocking detoxification elixirs.

What you will use is what is typically accessible to you every day at your local grocery store and perhaps even in your cupboards. Above all, the most important instrument you will use is: your body.

The 30-Day Wellness Alchemist Detox is both a *physical* and a *mental* detox. It will introduce you to a cleanse that invites you to step out of the current illusion you may be stuck in — to become aware, sensitively and honestly, of the intimate nature of your habits and how your relationship with yourself, your body and your surroundings affects your eating habits.

This guidebook may be used as a written companion to help you unlock the doors to life, as you want it to be.

How do you live life to the fullest?

You can start by developing a conscious connection with your body instead of merely following what is dictated by the habitual thinking, over-analyzing mind. You can start to learn how to nourish your body honestly and intuitively by becoming aware of what it truly needs – by sensing it, acknowledging it and responding to it.

Throughout this detox, you will be encouraged to replace your unhealthy habits with life-enhancing new ones.

When we begin to let go of the trauma of the past and the worries of the future, when we start to observe rather than fight, resist or unconsciously respond to the habits of our thinking mind, we learn to recognize that our mind is not against us. On the contrary, our mind can be a powerful ally in the escape from the unhealthy habitual cycles that we get stuck in. The practice of awareness can help us become an observer to such habitual mind patterns, sensitive to the effects they have on the quality of our lives and honest to how we approach a way out.

It can seem like there is no hope, that the mind is a battle we'll never win. But there is hope and you have what it takes to evolve into a whole, more alive and aware version of you.

Although it may not seem so at all times, we are always in the midst of our greatest work. And, even in times of what feels like a relentless lack of motivation and inspiration or on the contrary, in times of extreme busyness and stress, we hold the ability to tap into our body's wisdom. Life is irrevocably supporting us — in the easiest and toughest of times — and our bodies are the greatest instruments we have to experience it.

What is Alchemy?

Simply put, *Alchemy* is *Transformation*.

In antiquity, the term Alchemy referred to a sacred, mystical and more holistic understanding of science, through which Alchemists transformed base metals (iron, lead) into noble metals (gold or silver). Alchemists also tried to develop an elixir of life that would confer longevity and youth.

We believe that the concept of Alchemy as Transformation, in its broader sense, illustrates the *magical*, *sacred* and *holistic* process of change and healing that takes place in each one of us, when we start regarding and treating ourselves as a whole, rather than trying to cure and change different parts of us or our lives based on preconceived ideas and other *shoulds*, *musts* or *have-tos* that we've been trained to believe without questioning.

When we approach the mystery of us from a beginner's/unprecedented/objective state of wonder and attitude of surrender, we can slowly learn how to listen to our intuition – our still small voice we've been ignoring for most of our life – and over time, we become our best ally. We also free ourselves from the outside, imposed idea of what we should be, do, eat or have and we start re-creating our own life, in accordance with our own uniqueness and deepest purpose.

Thus, once we start getting reacquainted with our true selves, we begin a lifetime of alchemy – a deep, holistic transformation, from the inside out. We learn to prepare and drink our own existential elixir, which will help us live the life we love and love the life we live, more deeply, awake and aware.

No one knows your better than you. No one can change or save you. No one can truly heal you. Only you. You are both, the key and the door to you. You are your best doctor and friend.

All the answers to our deepest secrets are contained within ourselves. And so is the power to heal ourselves from our deepest wounds and re-create a life worth living. As Alchemists of our own lives, our highest hope through this Wellness Alchemy process is to re-acquaint you with your own Interdependent Republic of You – to help you become, in turn, your own Alchemist and Healer, the master of your body and mind, the artist of your life and creator of your destiny.

We begin this process with the most tangible, literal and approachable practice: the Art of Feeding Ourselves. Our nourishment goes beyond food, but food has a direct passage into our bodies and it acts at the most basic level of our transformation: it is assimilated and converted by our body into direct pieces of us – our cells and functions – which in turn, affect the intangible areas: our emotions, our state of mind, our relationships, our mood and our overall health and well-being.

Whether you've realized, accepted and embraced this fact, or not, you have the power to transform and to create. Connecting with the cellular response of your inner being to the way in which you nourish yourself with food is the very first step. Your body was created to support your evolution, but you must learn to support your body. Your body has the wisdom to move towards balance and you have what it takes to tap into its essence. As you were born with the ability of an alchemist, you are naturally a master of transformation, the way of creation. Once you embrace this great work as alchemist and conscious creator, you become the ultimate artist of your life.

This detox...

The 30-day Wellness Alchemist Detox is not about subtracting your negative habits or denying your simple unhealthy food pleasures. It is a process of transformation during which you will learn to re-calibrate the mind and body connection so that you are able to tap into the wisdom of your life-vessel in order to nourish it in a way that is life-giving — where this pleasure grows beyond your current imagination.

This detox is about the abundance that begins with an honest, sincere conversation between your body and you. Perhaps it will be the first real conversation you've ever had or perhaps it will help you clarify and strengthen your ongoing dialogue with your body. Either way, you are far from alone. Our whole society structure is built in such a way as to distract us from having intimate conversation with ourselves. Massive, profitable industries focus on influencing all of us to place artificial beauty above our health. This detox invites you to change superficial belief into a deep and meaningful practice, to make healthy beautiful and allow inner beauty to shine through your optimal health and well-being.

This detox is not about psychoanalyzing your childhood, your trauma, or whatever made you the person you are today. You simply cannot be anyone other than who you are in the present, no matter what type of past shaped you into you.

This detox will invite you to acknowledge, feel and release stored pain, resistance, anger, disillusion, lack of forgiveness, self-doubt and all the other negative factors keeping you from listening to your body. This detox will also invite a space for you to release the false illusions that you carry about yourself — whether you've assigned these to yourself from life experiences or were assigned to you by others, you'll be invited to let go of what no longer serves you in a way that is safe and most optimal for you.

When it's time to make a significant change, we tend to over-analyze or even make life-altering decisions based on our past. However, a precise articulation of past experiences that caused anguish and pain is not necessarily a prerequisite to healing, changing or moving on. We don't have to relive the trauma that we experienced in the past over and over. We just have to sincerely and lovingly acknowledge its presence in our bodies and stop trying not to feel it. We can become aware of the perpetual patterns we constantly relive – mentally and physically – that keep us stagnant and disillusioned. Acknowledging these patterns, even in the slightest, opens a door of opportunity to take the steps that best suit us to release, create space and to tap into the wisdom that we are.

It all comes down to how we treat ourselves. One of the most common ways to self-destruct and to lose touch with our bodies is through food and overall nourishment, whether it is by eating unhealthy food or by eating too little or too much food.

This detox is about inviting sensitivity, awareness and honesty into the way you eat, digest and prepare food as well as what you choose to eat.

This detox is about allowing new doors to open and letting your mind and body embark on a more spacious, livelier, more sincere and more conscious adventure.

It is about recognizing your patterns at the same time as you acknowledge your body, the connection with your mind and heart, and use this new paradigm to invite a release of all the blockages holding you back.

The goal of this detox is to empower you to recalibrate your relationship with yourself, with your mind and with your body through your connection with your nourishment in order to develop sincere, intuitive habits that invite your diet choices to become self-empowering, liberating, confidence-boosting, nourishing, healing and energetically optimal as opposed to cyclical, negative, energy-draining and ultimately life-long struggles.

What are the rules of this detox?

There are no specific rules because deep down you already know what is good for you and what isn't. Tapping into that knowledge and discovering what is truly nourishing for your body has the potential to make you feel more alive than any other prescribed diet possibly could.

Tuning into your own truth is more liberating and more effective than blind faith in what works for others. Life doesn't come with a standard manual. Neither do you. But you do come into this world with the necessity and ability to create your own manual in order to become the best and most alive version of what you already are.

The detox process.

This guidebook is intended to help you discover yourself by applying layers of mindfulness to your life with the use of inspirational tools such as a daily self-care routine and keeping a daily food, exercise & experience journal.

The first layer will invite the recovery of your awareness. Awareness helps release us from deep imprinted habits. It offers a tremendous amount of depth and has a profound transformative potential for not only the way in which we nourish ourselves with food, but in all aspects of life. Awareness is also an invitation toward wholeness versus focusing solely on separate parts or aspects of us, or only inviting the idea of awareness into certain activities such as yoga class, meditation or practicing your craft, and then 'turning it off' again once the effort ceases.

Cultivating awareness also takes time, courage and a willingness to truly see and observe who and what we are. It is not a button we can simply press and 'turn on' to retrieve sudden results but a wisdom that takes practice.

Awareness can also be described as acquiring the ability to hear all of our inner voices objectively and to not necessarily live out the stories they tell, the labels they assign, or to have an incessant discussion and argument or negotiation with them. The key is to discover the conditioning that exists within these voices — the conditioning that keeps us from waking up to the reality of being alive.

Through awareness we can begin to understand why our suffering occurs and eventually we can become able to change negative reoccurring patterns. Instead of being carried away by thought after thought, awareness guides us toward unlimited wisdom, expansion and nourishment.

Awareness is allowing You to happen. It will help you organize thought patterns and manage your time, resulting in a less cluttered mind and more time to invite a state of pure presence into your life. You'll have more clarity to become aware of the food and nourishment choices you are making, as well as of the state of mind you are in while making them. This routine is meant to help you bring lasting confidence and space to your life.

The second layer will invite the recovery of your sensitivity. The building of sensitivity helps us consciously reclaim our bodies. The first step is learning to feel, as clearly as we can, the effects of how we currently nourish ourselves with food and with the life around us. This practice will also reveal patterns that have been stored and remembered by the body — deep emotions, trauma and, most likely, false beliefs we've held about who and what we are.

The development of sensitivity also takes time, since many of us are experts at numbing ourselves to emotional distress and not feeling the parts of us that we've deemed imperfect, unlovable, tainted or unworthy.

So, although at times this process of feeling deeply can seem extremely challenging, it is important to know that all you need is a willingness to *tune in and to feel more*, and even the smallest sincere effort will tap into a deeper knowingness. You'll realize that not all of it can be articulated. Instead, it will manifest itself as an inner intuitive realization.

As awareness, the development of sensitivity is a life-long practice, in which one layer will reveal itself, followed by another, and so on. The more you discover and acknowledge, the greater the consciousness of your body will become and the more empowered you will feel.

What you discover won't always be easy. Sadness, loneliness, anger and trauma stored in your body can be difficult to face if you are in the habit of fighting, denying or resisting these emotions (pushing them deeper into your body) instead of dealing with them consciously and honestly.

However, if you can acknowledge these emotions as habits – as mere imprints of memories in your body – and at the same time recognize that there is nothing wrong with you because they are there, you can make it possible for you to release them in your own way without any force or danger.

You don't have to keep carrying around what no longer serves you, and allowing these obstacles to surface enables you to begin using them as a tool to understand who you are.

This second layer is an invitation to free yourself by feeling your body and thus opening up to understanding the dialect of your emotions through the gentle acknowledgement of your habits.

Feeling beyond the surface of your emotions can also open you up to discovering a deep self-love and acceptance for who and what you are in the present moment, no matter how you got here.

You don't have to keep holding onto regret, anger or disappointment if you want to move on. It's not to say you won't experience these emotions again, but you can make them less dominating in your life. Contrary to the autopilot reaction, you'll be able to respond with a more mindful approach where anger, fear and disappointment are slower to arise.

Every new ounce of awareness and sensitivity accompanied with self-love, respect and acceptance can increase your ability to make outstanding life decisions.

The third and last layer of the process is recovering your Honesty. Honesty is a layer that can be extremely difficult, as most of us live within a mind and a society of little white lies, illusions and disillusions. We tell ourselves that it's okay to do things that we know aren't deeply nourishing. The lies keep the seemingly self-destructive side of our egos happy and our unhealthy habits strong.

We lie to ourselves about our ability to change, love, move on, forgive, etc. We also lie to ourselves about how we are feeling, what is actually happening in our bodies, our lives, or what the food we consume is doing to our bodies, and we relentlessly try to control or force the present moment to happen in a way that justifies our unhealthy habits.

You are not alone in this. We are all players in this game.

With even the smallest effort of sincere honesty, you can start building a foundation for a new perspective, gain a glimpse at your real beauty and embrace it all as healthy ammunition to keep going and to keep discovering who you are.

We all have that little voice inside our heads – the voice that criticizes, judges, assigns descriptive words toward what we believe are our limitations, and it is never pleased with our performance. Perhaps with honesty we can invite that voice to soften as we start to truly honor our bodies and lives by the way we choose to nourish them. And as that voice transforms from self-destructive to supportive, we can begin to realize our potential and invite ourselves to *show up* in our daily endeavors, materializing the beautiful and powerful inherent gifts we possess.

Let's get real and be as honest with ourselves as we possibly can.

Honesty also comes in layers. The more you practice it, the clearer you will be able to see the destructive patterns in your life, and the closer you'll get to doing something about them.

Honesty is empowerment. It strengthens your integrity and it comes with no strings attached. It cancels out everything and it requires no extensive articulation or esoteric description. It is a path of expansion and fulfillment – of creating space and balance within and without.

Why is food a central issue?

In a more general aspect, food is nourishment. More than just food, every single thing you put in your body – and your mind – is either nourishing you or depleting you of perspective, truth, vitality, energy and thus, your vital nutrients.

Thoughts, ideas, conversations, experiences, relationships, work, television and newspapers – everything you open your life to counts as nourishment.

Yet, what you eat is the most specific and literal form of nourishment. It affects you in a direct way, because through digestion food turns into nutrients that feed and grow cells that, in turn, maintain and build the body and mind.

The saying "You are what you eat" is literally true. The body has the ability to transform food into visible pieces of us. You are what you eat on all levels, starting at a most fundamental, simple one: your cells.

Eating is one of our main vital functions, essential to our survival, but it is not automatic. It requires you to use your decision-making ability. Your heart beats to its own drum. Your lungs breathe without requesting permission. Your blood pumps consistently and automatically through your body.

Eating demands and even begs for the use of intellect – nowadays more than ever. And we won't be our full and optimal selves, unless we design and adapt our own, personalized eating habits instead of limiting ourselves to an automatic nurturing process inherited through culture, family and education.

Our awakening begins when we start owning up to our *decision-making* ability and our *response*-ability – our capability to address life as intuitive, empowered and creative individuals. Since we can only experience our metaphysical realm through our physical bodies, this awakening won't take place until we begin to re-evaluate what we put into our bodies.

All our parts are created equal. There is no greater achievement on earth than following your call to be whole, reuniting all your powers under the same roof, in a life-house created and maintained by yourself – this house, your body.

Eating intelligently is an intuitive skill that the body possesses naturally, though it has been dulled by decades of negative habits passed down from generation to generation for many of us. These habits have warped our relationship with food, the preparation of it, food as part of our social interaction, food as an ingredient in our relationship with ourselves, our choice of diet and how we come to choose it. But we can change. Each one of us can choose to venture onto a journey that serves us in the best way possible no matter where we are at in our life. The rewards of such a path are worth it.

The benefits of eating healthy:
- Builds a strong immune system that protects your body better from illness.
- It is anti-inflammatory, good for joints and reduces puffiness and bloating.
- Helps with premature aging.
- Helps eliminate excess weight, cellulite and toxins.
- Promotes healthy skin, teeth, hair and bones.
- Helps develop healthy confidence and self-acceptance.
- Encourages stronger nutritional decision-making abilities and a deeper connection with the body.
- Helps nurture brain cells, clarifies a foggy mind, better focus, enhances motivation and creativity.
- Provides more energy.

Eating healthy may seem like travelling to a new country at first. You need to replace the language you are fluent in, with a new one – a language that you don't quite understand and which doesn't make immediate sense.

This may be confusing and even frustrating at first. No change comes easy, even a change for the better. But if you stick to it, with a sincere determination, patience and persistence, you will soon learn new "words" in this foreign language, which will then turn into sentences, then paragraphs, and finally, new patterns of thought and association.

One day you will wake up and realize that you can think and articulate all of your thoughts in this language. Your words will flow out naturally. Your body will slowly start to communicate with your nourishment, to naturally ask you for healthier options, and you will have the most nourishing *conversations* with your food (and with yourself). It's not that the body isn't asking you now – it's just that you may not be hearing it. Your ability to listen to your body's deepest needs for nourishment has been numbed out by the noise of the self-destructive, addictive eating patterns you've been bombarded with your whole life.

But once you renew your relationship with your food and start listening to your body and begin to speak your body's ancient language of wisdom, you'll realize that this is actually your mother tongue. You were born speaking and understanding it, but somewhere along your journey society, education, family and different addictions got in the way and over the years, you forgot.

You have been driven away from Nature (your real mother) and forced to learn a new language that has nothing to do with who you are. You have been a prisoner in a foreign land that is not your home, as much as you've been taught to believe so. You can see signs of discomfort in the way your body reacts to it. Something (or everything?) is not right...You've never quite fit in.

But you can come back home. You are only a slave of your paradigm and habits, as long as you agree to it. The only way you can learn a new language is...by speaking it; by getting fully and deeply immersed in it; by getting silent and listening to the ancient truth your body is whispering to you.

You can't wait until you know more or wait until you feel you are more prepared. Just take the first step now. You have to start before you're ready. Readiness increases as you practice being present. The only time is Now.

Wherever you are on your journey – whether you are aware of how food affects you and others, or you have just begun to explore the result of your diet – join us in this 30-day basic recovery of our nourishment capacity and power of choice, leading us to life-affirming transformation.

Behind the scenes of our unhealthy eating habits.

More often than not, poor eating habits represent (or have represented) turmoil in your life: stress, sadness, boredom, harbored anger, resentment or suppressed emotions. We resist the feeling of such turmoil and will often use food to self-medicate with either *too much* or *not enough*.

All of this is being recorded by the body and its trillions of cells. All of our experiences, both delightful and painful, are relentlessly being recorded.

Food is one of the most popular painkillers for emotional pains. By preoccupying the body and mind with food, we avoid going beyond the surface of these emotions and instead we push them away and numb ourselves by focusing on the perceived short-term pleasure and distraction we get from food.

Logically, we all know that this is not a long-term solution. The answers we seek are not written at the bottom of an extra-large cheese pizza box. Bad eating habits will only lead to further physical or emotional problems. But emotions are not often logical and as a consequence neither are our food choices.

Food gives us life, and it should not function as a painkiller but as a pain-healer.

The habitual cycle of shutting down emotions instead of facing them not only creates unhealthy side effects in our physical body (e.g. unnecessary weight gain, bloating, constipation, skin issues and even sickness and disease), it also holds us back mentally. Being stuck is an emotional, unreasonable state. The mind is almost as palpable as the body.

These cycles and mental blockages keep us from showing up 100% in our lives. Consider how many times you have turned to food to fix your mood, fill up the space left by *loneliness* or *rejection*. Consider how many times you've cancelled a date, a meeting with a friend or plans of going to a party because you didn't feel ready or good enough to make the effort, and instead stayed at home to eat. Consider how often sad or angry emotions have brought you to make choices enabling you to maintain unhealthy eating habits and leaving you uninterested in the life around you or yourself.

Think about how long these food fixes have lingered in your life.

Your mind has the ability to hold you captive in an unhealthy cycle if you allow negative habits in to infiltrate your relationship with food.

Filling the body with junk food and expecting to feel good is a bit like trying to fill up your car with soda pop and expecting it to work. The only difference is that junk food can momentarily silence your pain, but it won't heal it. The pain will come back later and if you continue this pattern, health problems will be added to your pain.

Food can be a nurturing source of energy for the greatest instrument we have to experience this life – our body – or it can be a poisonous trap with a negative effect on our self-perception, how we interact in relationships, how we spend our time, the lifestyle choices we make and what career we choose. It can also impact how *free* we feel within our lives versus how *trapped* we are in the false notions, preconceptions and ideas about our lives. And it can keep you from having the courage to make the necessary choices for you to be who you truly are.

There is a tremendous amount of authentic and sincere beauty in being healthy, and great joy, new possibilities, as well as a meaningful mindset will come along with it.

All it takes is a sincere and consistent effort to improve your nourishment. This will bring about a significant opportunity to heal yourself and impact your life in profound ways.

The only real requirement for this detox is a willingness to become as intimate as possible with the way your nurture yourself and to allow – not force – the natural wisdom of your body to shine through.

Become your own friend, teacher and healer. Get to really know yourself. Listen closely to what's happening within and develop a genuine love and kindness for your true and unique wonder.

Why do we eat what we eat?

Most of what we eat is not necessarily natural or healthy but a result of our culture, our traditions, our education and other socially determined factors. Just like the rest of our body, our taste buds are flexible. They adjust. Man is a creature of habit but also the most adaptable of creatures.

When it comes to our food, we've simply been trained to eat a certain way and (often unintentionally) taught to love certain foods. Most of our ideas of "good" and "bad" tastes are acquired while growing up – typically in the first decade of our life, when most life-lasting impressions are registered. That is also when we develop emotional attachments to food – both healthy and unhealthy ones.

Being fed candy, fast food and soda pop as children often come as a reward or as recognition from our parents. As we age, we often fill our need for acknowledgement and recognition in the same way.

On the inside, we all share the same structure. The body is an extremely intelligent organism. It is equipped with the power to recreate, readapt, reshape and restructure itself and it will make-do with what it gets or has until it can no longer run efficiently. It inherently knows what is good for it and what isn't, but it can only work with whatever we use to nourish it.

Each of us is born with the innate ability to tap into the intelligence of our bodies in order to understand what we need in order to heal and to nourish ourselves. Yes, you have the ability and power to heal yourself better than anyone else can ever do for you.

What should we eat?

Every person is different and we each have unique needs. No one diet fits all. What may work great for one, may not work for another.

When in doubt, there are some general healthy suggestions and food focus groups you can refer to. We share 99.9% of our DNA, after all. Although unique, our needs can't be that far off from one another. We just have to find the right chemistry that works optimally for our own bodies. So, our nourishment may differ from one person to another but we all share a similar basis.

The equation is simple. We are Nature. So we must eat Nature. We need to get as close to nature as possible, in every aspect, especially when it comes to what we put in our bodies. We all need fresh, organically grown food, free of chemicals, pesticides, drugs and genetic modifications. We all need food that our bodies can naturally recognize and assimilate – and not have to fight off.

So, what should humans eat? We suggest real, whole, fresh and natural food – not some plastic, chemicalized, addictive and damaging version of it. And we should try to make getting this food a priority, whatever our circumstances.

We must use our creative power to do what we can, with what we have, right here and right now. Remember, we can't wait until we're ready. Ready is a state of mind, not a single moment or a set of circumstances.

As a strong, healthy basis for your diet, we recommend that you begin to practice a nourishing relationship with the following food groups. Get acquainted with new healthy foods and add more of these life-giving nutrients to your daily meals. As often as possible, try to get seasonal and local foods.

Foundational Foods (Eat Generously)

Leafy Greens	Lettuce, Spinach, Arugula, Kale, Collards, Broccoli, Mustard Greens, Cabbage, Brussels Sprouts, Dandelion, Turnip, Chard...
Fruits	Apples, Berries, Oranges, Pears, Bananas, Mangos, Grapes, Pomegranates, Papayas, Figs, Kiwi, Grapefruit, Lemon, Watermelon...
Vegetables	Carrots, Squash, Celery, Sweet Potato, Bell Pepper, Garlic, Onions, Asparagus, Cucumber, Fennel, Beets, Tomatoes, Eggplant, Cauliflower, Avocados...

Fresh Fruit & Vegetable Juices and Smoothies.

Proteins & Amino-Acids Source Foods (Eat Moderately)

Sprouts	Alfalfa, Lentil, Fenugreek, Chickpea, Beet Seeds...
Legumes	Beans, Peas, Lentils, Chickpeas, Edamame...
Whole Grains	Brown Rice, Spelt, Quinoa, Oats, Millet, Amaranth, Barley, Kamut, Buckwheat...
Nuts	Walnuts, Almonds, Hazelnuts, Brazil nuts, Pine nuts, Cashews, Pecans...
Seeds	Sesame, Flax, Hemp, Chia, Sunflower, Pumpkin...

Medicinal Foods (Eat Sparingly)

Algae	Spirulina, Chlorella, Nori, Dulse, Wakame...
Herbs & Spices	Ginger, Mint, Parsley, Oregano, Cumin, Turmeric, Rosemary, Cinnamon, Cayenne...
Microgreens	Arugula, Cilantro, Basil, Beet Leaves, Daikon Radish...
Cold-pressed Oils	Coconut, Sesame, Flaxseed, Grape Seed, Olive Oil...

What is your inner talk before, during and after a meal? Food is the most direct, sensory way to assess your inner talk. You could say that how you approach your plate is similar to how you approach life – how you hold your fork can be said to reflect the way you grasp your negative habits.

Tips for eating mindfully (that is, with your mind first):
- Breathe between bites.
- Eat when you're hungry.
- Stop eating when you're full.
- Don't take more than you need (or can eat).
- Take less / order less.
- Take the time to feel the state of your belly, your energy levels, your mood.
- Acknowledge the flavors and tastes your pallet prefers.
- Don't be afraid to say: enough is enough.

The day before.

The mind can do crazy things when you invite the possibility of looking through a different lens, such as starting a detox. Many of us experience the *one last time* effect – the mind convincing you to eat all your fried, sugar-flavored and unhealthy favorites *one last time*, before your detox begins. How many times have you had one last indulgence? We've all been there.

The relentless trap of promise-making and starting tomorrow.

When in times of weakness, notice the promises that the mind makes. When it talks you into making an unhealthy choice with the promise of never repeating it, know that you are already making the path even steeper. These are creative ways the mind uses to go back to what it is used to – its cycle of negative habits.

How do you overcome this mindset? We recommend trying not to force, control or to make any definitive promises to your self – and, try not to preconceive or predict outcomes. Also, try to remain *vigilant, sincere and consistent* – keep going no matter what.

The idea is not to force yourself into a new way of eating or thinking about your food, but to allow the change to be natural – to tap into your body's wisdom and generate results based on consistent effort, allowing you to become aware of your relationship with food, sensitive to the effects it has on your body and to let mindfulness deepen on an honest and meaningful level.

The change must first happen on the inside. That is where true power lies and where your life-driving force is found. From there, it will flow to all other areas of your life.

Through the next 30 days we won't be hacking at the leaves (your circumstances, actions, negative habits, etc.). We'll try to strike the root instead (your inner core and your beliefs about life). That is where magic happens, through the full use of our power of choice and innate ability to change. Once we get to the root and remove what doesn't serve, we'll have new space to fill – and with proper nourishment, new, healthier roots will grow and extend their branches into all other areas of our life.

In order to get below the surface you must make your way through the first layers. Somewhere within all that wiring and packaging is an extraordinary you.

The following *Detox Ambitions* will help you clear the way. You can personalize them to fit your own day. When it begins to seem impossible or unrealistic, remember that it's only 30 days. You can put up with anything for 30 days, especially that which might just change your life for the better.

Remember, you know what is best for you more than anyone else. Be kind to yourself and accept that even the revealing of this knowledge takes time.

The following are suggestions and not rules for how and where to get started. None of these ambitions or guidelines should be treated as a rigid regime, but as a starting point for exploration and discovery. No matter what, try to relax into this process. May it be a nourishing offering and a profound opportunity to tap into the wisdom of You.

	What?	Why?
Getting Started:	• Clean out your refrigerator. Throw away old and expired products. Take out all the food and clean the shelves. • Do the same as above, but with your cupboards. • Clean up the rest of your living space. • Donate items you don't need anymore. • Change your sheets.	To create outside what you'd like to create inside.
Daily Ambitions:	• Try to get enough rest. • If you don't already, experiment with going to bed early and waking up early. How about an hour before sunrise or at sunrise and an hour after sunset, depending on where you are in the world? If this is not achievable, do the best you can. • Exercise at least 30 minutes per day, six days per week. • Explore eating 2-3 healthy meals per day (not in front of the TV, PC, laptop or any other screen). • Forget about scales. • Avoid fast food, processed food or canned food. • Limit gluten (e.g. white bread, pasta, etc.) • Avoid pastries, cakes, cookies, high fructose corn syrup, sugar, artificial sweeteners, additives, flavor enhancers, etc. • Limit the amount of red meat, poultry and fish (or try to go completely without meat for 30 days). • Limit the amount of coffee you're drinking per day – how about 1-2 cups in the early morning only? Go for tea in the afternoon, if necessary. • Limit the amount of dairy products (or try to go completely without dairy for 30 days). • Avoid soda, including diet soda. • Avoid snacking between meals unless absolutely necessary. If so, make a healthy choice. • Increase your intake of whole foods: fruit, vegetables, grains, leafy-greens, legumes, nuts and seeds. • Drink a lot of water, herbal tea and fresh juices.	To add structure to your detox and support yourself – body, mind and heart – through this process as optimally as possible.

Will this really work?

If you find yourself thinking that this will never work and wondering what the trick is, we ask you to take a step forward in faith, give this an honest and sincere 30-day effort and see what happens. If you stay awake and aware, you may just be surprised by the transformative impact these 30 days will have on your entire life.

To tell or not to tell.

Don't be afraid to tell people that you are going to start a detox and don't be afraid to keep it to yourself either. Simply be aware of why you are doing either. If you are not telling because you are afraid of failure, then perhaps tell someone you trust and who will support you.

Try not to let anyone's criticism or lack of belief get in your way. Dealing with external resistance means recognizing that we are all on a path that is challenging at times, but learning to deal with such resistance more objectively and with detached compassion will help.

Believe in yourself. Know that what you are doing is for the empowerment and discovery of your true self and not for anyone else (although many will benefit from your efforts).

Time is of the essence.

When we initiate a detox we can become very conscious of the element of time and how little of it we seem to have or how long it's going to take to reap any benefits. This is another mental block that can be gently recalibrated in order to allow change to happen. Alleviating this barrier helps us become aware of what is actually taking place in our lives. Try not to stress about the notion of time and allow things to happen naturally, without force or control. Trust that everything is being revealed at a pace that you have chosen — one that is best suited for you.

Acknowledge that the moment you decide to change, you already have. Keep reminding yourself of this. Change is already happening and you already hold the benefits, the knowledge and tools to be who and what you are.

We all have very full schedules, but there is also a good chance that half the things we do on a daily basis can be prioritized differently or even let go of completely. The next time you catch yourself thinking that *you don't have enough time for this detox*, use it as a confirmation to stick with it.

If not now, when?

You have time to do what is best for you, no matter how busy you might to be. The mind is quite creative when making excuses and we more than often give in to them. Becoming aware of the distractions is the first step toward not reacting to them.

Start by setting the intention of being sincere with yourself. Try to find the joy in taking the time to do what is good for you. This may mean that you set healthy boundaries like getting up earlier, going to bed earlier and cutting out some television time in order to relax, exercise or prepare your meals. Instead of fighting it, try this exploration with open arms.

Remember that no one is making you do anything. This process is truly up to you — it's yours and yours alone. And *Now* is not just the right time to begin, but the *only* time we'll ever have.

The daily routine.

This is what a typical day could look like, whether it's a workday or not. Throughout your first 30 days, this guidebook will provide you with daily motivators, focus areas, reminders, ideas, inspiration and space for you to express your experience.

But first, let's get into some pre-detox details...

A note about serving size.

There is a pretty good chance that you have been eating more than you need to, so as a rule of thumb, make your servings smaller (you can always get more later) and stop eating when you feel the first signs of being full. This could take practice, so be patient with yourself.

At first, it may not be easy to feel if you are full or not, but keep allowing for sensitivity to open up into the space of your belly. Your sensitivity will improve as you become more aware of the signals your body is sending. Soon you will be able to observe what is happening and respond in a conscious and healthy way.

Remember, you know what is best for you more than anyone else. The following are suggestions – not rules – for how and where to get started. These guidelines are not to be treated as a rigid regime, but only as a starting point for exploration and discovery. No matter what, relax into this process, as it is deeply nourishing for your body.

Daily Schedule – for inspiration

Morning (Rise to Lunch)

- Wake up (and get out of bed) early. Try 6 a.m. or 1 hour before sunrise.
- Lie still in bed or find a place to sit quietly for at least 5-10 minutes – just relax, breathe and try not to converse with the voices in your mind.
- Exercise for at least 30 minutes — doing it first thing in the morning helps avoid all the excuses that can present themselves later in the day.
- Drink water. Warm water with a few lemon drops will help increase alkalinity and help with elimination.
- Shower/bathe.
- Eat a light breakfast within 30-45 minutes of waking up (unless you exercise first). We recommend eating after (rather than before) you exercise.
- Do not skip breakfast (eat without TV, phone, or other distractions).

Lunch (Noonish)

- Make/pack your own lunch if there are no healthy and nutritious options available at work.
- Be with your food — try not to work, surf, text or talk on the phone.
- Try to take a light walk in the fresh air after eating.
- Remember to drink plenty of water, herbal tea or fresh vegetable/fruit juice during the afternoon but also have space in your day when you aren't drinking or consuming constantly.
- If you exercise over your lunch hour, we recommend exercising before eating lunch. However, it is preferable to do your exercise routine in the morning, if possible.

Dinner (4-6 pm)

- Keep it light. This isn't a good time of day to go overboard or to indulge. Your metabolism, your whole body in fact, begins to slow down at this time of day, as you only have a few waking hours left. Sleep is an important time for the body to refuel, detox and rehabilitate. If you spend this time digesting, there is a chance you won't feel optimal in the morning.
- If you exercise in the evening, we recommend that you do so before dinner or a sufficient amount of time after your light dinner so the body has time to digest. However, it is preferable to do your exercise routine in the morning, if possible.
- Take time to relax, connect with yourself, your family, pets and friends.

Tips for getting a good night's rest:
- Shower or bathe before bed.
- Try not to work, engage in work-related or stressful activities at least two hours before sleep.
- Try not to drink a lot at least two hours before sleep and especially no caffeine.
- Sit or lie down for at least 2-5 minutes at the end your day (you can also do this while in bed). Take this time to just breathe, relax, detach from your schedule, to-do list and the clock. Soul-search and/or meditate.
- Do your daily self-check before bed or after dinner (to be discussed in the following pages).
- Note: You may not be used to going to bed early, but it will soon become natural as you create a new routine for yourself. Your body will adjust your sleeping hours aided by your new habits.

The very first step: getting out of bed in the morning.

Perhaps you're used to getting up early in the morning, perhaps not. Either way, waking up early provides you with the time to do things at a calmer pace, which can drastically impact the quality of the rest of your day. The early morning hours are usually the best time of day to enjoy some peaceful quiet time, especially if you live in a full house, and it is the best moment to set the tone for the rest of your day.

Note: The very first thing you do in the morning has the power to influence the quality of the rest of your day.

Set your alarm clock and get out of bed before you have time to convince yourself to stay under your warm blankets. When you begin to negotiate with yourself – "five more minutes" or "I have time for another snooze if I cut my shower short" or "I'll get up early tomorrow" – you make the hill a hell of a lot steeper than it already is. So do yourself a huge favor and just get up when you hear the alarm. No snooze, no excuses, no negotiation. Just do.

What to do if you aren't feeling well.

If you truly aren't feeling well, do what is best for your body, but be honest with yourself. Our excuses can get extremely creative when we don't feel like exercising, getting out of bed or sticking to our positive routines. Feeling even just a little bit off can make it very difficult to dig deep and find the strength, energy and positive attitude to stick with it.

So listen to your body and decide with sincerity whether you'll benefit from reaching deep and sticking with your new routine or if you really need more rest to get better. Either way, as long as you make an honest choice, your body will thank you for it later.

Inspirational tips for a daily routine.

These tips aren't limited to the times prescribed. They are arranged like this to help you organize your time in a way that works best for you. Eventually, you will be comfortable using all of these at various times throughout your day.

What could support or inhibit you?

Morning (gently) suggested tips:

What could support you:

- Go to the bathroom. Brush your teeth. Splash water on your face.

- Do some form of exercise. Exercising first thing in the morning while your body is still waking up will give you extra energy throughout the day. You will naturally move slower, more cautiously and hopefully without a whole lot of chatter in the mind, and because the body is naturally stiffer in the morning, you'll start to gain more awareness of your tight spots without trying to force your body to do something it may not be ready for in the early hours of the day. Exercising first thing in the morning also gets it out of the way. You can spend the rest of the day feeling good about it. If you wait until later in the day, something else might interfere and make way for excuses to not doing it at all.

What could inhibit you:

- Try not to get on the computer, check emails or text messages until after you've eaten/exercised/showered. Better yet, wait until you get to work.

- Try not to talk on the phone or engage in *heavy* conversation in the morning. If possible, don't talk at all until after you've spent some quiet time with yourself and had your breakfast.

- Try not to skip breakfast and do not work, watch television or talk on the phone while eating.

Lunchtime (gently) suggested tips:

What could support you:

- Drink plenty of water or fresh juice before lunch. Don't wait until you are sitting down to eat. Hydrate yourself between meals, but don't feel like you constantly have to be drinking something. Sooner or later, you will be able to tell when the body requires hydration and when it requires sustenance.

- Give yourself enough time to choose something healthy to eat and enough time to eat and digest it.

- Before heading out to lunch, especially if you are getting some kind of takeaway, give your choice an honest thought. Don't allow people around you to influence you negatively. Go solo if you have to. You won't regret it.

- Before eating, take a few seconds for gratitude. Acknowledge what it is and be grateful for the chain of people who made it possible for it to end up on your plate.

- Chew your food thoroughly and remember to breathe in between bites. Practice feeling the sensations of the food in your mouth, the fullness of your belly, the way you hold your fork and any emotions or intensity present before, during and after eating. Relax as much as you can while you eat.

- Go for a ten to fifteen minute walk after you eat. Invite a co-worker, neighbor, friend or family member or take some time to be alone. If you can't go for a walk, try to get some fresh air, even if it's just standing outside for a few moments.

- If you can, lie down for at least 15 minutes.

What could inhibit you:

- Try not to eat at your work desk, and don't eat while working. Never eat on the run or in a hurry.

- Try not to rush back to work. Everything can wait for your health.

- Try not to skip lunch.

- Try not to substitute – don't eat more for lunch if you were naughty and skipped breakfast and don't skip lunch if you plan on splurging on a big dinner.

- Try not engaging in stressful or negative conversations while eating.

- Try to avoid buffets, fast food and diners. If you do eat out, find a whole foods market or a place that serves fresh salads, soups and other choices you know are good for you.

Evening suggested Dos and Don'ts:

What could support you:

• Only eat if you're hungry.

• Eat as early in the evening as possible.

• Choose something light.

• Turn off all your electronics and appliances that can be unplugged at least one hour before bed. Electronics vibrate at a much higher frequency than our bodies. They become a source of stress and prevent your body from getting a full night's rest, increasing the risk for depression. Try to spend the last hour awake in a deep state of relaxation, unplugged from most sources of stress and distraction.

• Take time to journal, meditate and exercise for as long as you can in the evening. If you have trouble finding time for journaling, do it as the last thing before you go to sleep.

• Reading for pleasure right before bed helps you relax and invite sleep. Pick up a book you love and devour a few pages until sleep calls.

What could inhibit you:

• Don't be afraid to say "no thanks" to temptations.

• Try not to make excuses to go back to your old ways.

• Try not to eat right before bed or late at night.

• Try not to drink many fluids during your last hours awake. Excessive intake of fluids before bed disrupts your sleep.

Your Daily Detox Journal.

Your Daily Detox Journal is a way for you to track your progress, to make notes, and to journal about your experience. Writing supports your willingness to acknowledge what is actually happening. It makes you even more aware of the patterns in your life and it invites the elements of your sensitivity, your feelings, and your honesty to the equation.

Journaling will serve as a reflective mirror of your journey. By writing we not only de-clutter and detox our mind, we also reframe our life. We create space for new and healthier habits. We are given a chance to re-write our story.

Writing about your experiences – in free form, without any restrictions or expectations – helps you let go of extra mind debris, leaving more space for what really matters. It also puts your problems and worries into perspective and serves as a way of measuring your path, which will be helpful in the future as a reference point to the past, when inspiration regarding your process of change is needed.

Remember that you are doing this for you – to know yourself and to discover who you are beyond your habits. This wisdom is in you, but you may have buried it deep. Writing every day is a very important opportunity to practice honesty as well as to find the encouragement to keep going. This process of building awareness, sensitivity and honesty is an invitation to become more personal and intimate with you, which in itself can be a profound healing mechanism.

Tips for journaling:
- Don't hold back. Nobody will read your journal, unless you want them to. Go as deep and as personal as you need to. Write until your heart is content.
- Be honest.
- Try not to create perfection, but allow your expression to be the surface of a deeper impression of what is happening inside of you.
- If you need to write more, don't hold back – use a notebook or get additional paper.
- Don't judge yourself based on what you have written. Become a compassionate, detached observer to what comes out of you.
- Don't worry about your writing making sense, as this may stand in your way of clearing your mind. Nobody writes in this guidebook but you. The mind debris is what usually comes out first. The gold lies at the bottom. But in order to get to it, you need to dig through layers and layers of accumulated clutter. Don't be embarrassed by the nonsense when it shows up on paper. Through daily mental house cleaning, your thoughts will become clearer, you will be able to tap into your own source of wisdom and, with newfound confidence and experience, you'll get through the daily practice.

Inspiration for self-care.

For each of the next 30 days, you will find three sections of suggested self-care exercises adapted to each day. These are meant to provide actionable inspiration, daily support as well as space to record your experience through this transformative process.

This is your journey. Take these exercises as additional support to help you communicate better with yourself. Be as honest as possible in your annotations. And don't judge yourself. There is no right or wrong answer. There is only the process of becoming You – an imperfect, mysterious, alive and unique human being in constant transformation. The point is to become your own best friend and ally by first learning how to listen to and trust yourself.

Your daily annotations are divided in three sections:

1. The Daily Food & Exercise Diary.

Your Daily Food & Exercise Diary will help you invite the three key pillars of this detox – awareness, sensitivity and honesty – into the way you nourish yourself, through a gentle routine meant to create more space in your life, de-clutter your thoughts and make time for yourself.

Remember, you are your best friend and doctor. Check in with your body every day and get to know one another.

2. The Daily Love Box.

These extra body-care actions are proposed to you as inspiration for additional self-care and can be used as supplemental (but equally vital) practices to your life and this detox.

We understand there isn't always time to do things that make us feel really good, but inviting just one or two of these each day or week can help the mind, body and heart connect in the most profound ways.

Most importantly, these actions are meant to make you feel good and they are not to be done mindlessly or without the sweet intention of nourishing yourself. The moment you find yourself doing these things as part of your to-do list, come back to it at a time when you can give yourself your full attention. It will be worth it.

3. Suggested Journaling Exercise.

Each day is designed with a specific focus and inquiry questions and points of reflection as it pertains to the three layers (awareness, sensitivity and honesty), to initiate a profound conversation with yourself and help you go deeper into the parts of you that need extra care and healing.

By opening up your heart with yourself every day and answering these questions with honesty and kindness you will be practicing active listening and you will begin to understand yourself a little more. By putting into words the still small voice inside that is often unheard or ignored, you will engage in an intimate conversation with your body, heart and mind and start taking nourishing, creative action over your life.

An important note about the beginning, the middle and the never-ending journey.

When you first start to detox and you realize what you are actually taking on, the task can seem daunting. You might recall past experiences where you went overboard – times when you were sad or angry and used food as comfort. You may even have treated others badly in the process of an uncontrolled desire to indulge on the unhealthy.

You may not recognize that person in you. You may not want to. You may feel ashamed about it. It is not easy to fully acknowledge and accept the unpleasant sides of oneself. The best thing you can do is to forgive yourself and accept things as they are in the present. The past is an experience that guided you to this point in your life, where you are now ready to make a positive change.

It is equally important to recognize if you avoid your body. Once negative habits are confronted, veils are removed and you become exposed to yourself. We aren't always ready to see or feel the physical body we are in and the damage we may have done to it.

When you begin this detox, notice if you dislike (resist) parts of your body like your belly, your thighs, your hips, and your face. If you become aware of even the subtlest amount of resistance, try to replace that negativity with love. Try to accept all parts of your body, even the parts you've deemed ugly or inadequate. With this detox comes transformation, and chances are that you will discover an entirely new, empowered, balanced and beautiful you – a you that has always been there waiting to be acknowledged.

As you begin to unveil who you are, there will be times of confusion, and you will be challenged. These challenges are a goldmine, as they represent the really hard internal work that is being done. Your body, mind and heart are recalibrating and responding to your effort.

Remember, right now, right in this very moment, you are in the midst of your greatest, most sacred work: becoming your own healer and creative agent of change in your life.

And so it begins...

This is a process of building self-confidence. With practice and consistency, self-support, a healthy (non-rigid) routine and a desire for something better, you can begin to show up in life with full presence, sincerity and extraordinary love for yourself.

Let this journey bring a deep peace and healthy nourishment to your life so that, when times get rough, you will feel the loving awareness illuminating from within your body.

Let this be a reminder that you already have the tools to become who you truly are and that you have the wisdom, the strength and the power to make choices to change for the better.

Keep in mind that the goal of this detox isn't to change who you are, but to become aware of – and eventually let go of – the negative habits hiding the real you.

The following pages will provide you with a daily pep talk, reminders, ideas, mantras, inspiration, support and recommendations. As preparation and for inspiration, it may be a good idea to read each daily content the day before.

The insights for each day have been carefully selected. We want to address the key challenges of the mental re-building process that most of us typically go through when inviting a process of internal change – especially when dealing with negative habits.

Therefore, as previously discussed, we have sequenced the three focus areas to help you build Awareness, Sensitivity and Honesty.

The moment you decided to change, you already have. Once you realize this, you'll find it increasingly difficult to stay on the path of unhealthy habits.

"Awareness is the greatest alchemy there is. Just go on becoming more and more aware, and you will find your life changing for the better in every possible dimension. It will bring great fulfillment."

— Osho

FOCUS AREA I - AWARENESS

Key focal points:

- Develop an awareness of your attachments, habits and patterns in which you nourish yourself or lack nourishment.
- Become aware of the food choices you make.
- Become aware of the way you prepare and eat food.
- Become open to discovering the motives behind your food and nourishment choices.

Open your eyes. This is your life and there is so much more to experience than you think possible. You have only seen the tip of the iceberg.

The wisdom to make nourishing and life-affirming choices is contained within you: beauty and ugliness, darkness and light, joy and pain. Every answer to every question you have resides within. Inside is where you'll find the story of You. If you learn to read your own story, you'll also be able to rewrite it.

On the first ten days of this lifetime transformation, we will invite the possibility of looking deep within ourselves to discover who we are in a greater and more inclusive context.

Recognizing our self-destructive mind patterns is the first of many self-caring acts to come. Together, we'll attempt to observe the chatter of our minds and start distinguishing what is truthful and good for us from the unhealthy habits imposed by years on autopilot.

Day 1 - Awareness.

Mantra of the Day: "Until I run out of excuses, my life will never change."

You have to start somewhere. The idea is to simply go for it. Don't wait for something to happen. Don't wait for all the pieces to come together. You've been waiting for this moment, so take it. No more excuses.

Sure, the first step can seem daunting, but know that this doubt or fear is a normal part of the mental process. The habitual, un-awakened mind resists accepting the mystery of life nearly as much as it rejects change, so the more you keep vigilant, sincere and on the path of self-discovery, the easier it will be. It takes time and patience to be able to become aware of, feel, acknowledge; to hear our recurring constricting mind chatter and to break negative habits. So, try to stick with it. Doubt is just another obstacle on the road.

What made being healthy so hard in the first place? Years of excuses, blame, lack of forgiveness, disillusion, self-medicating and comfort eating can leave you in a state of ignorant bliss, preventing you from exploring the healing and expansive possibilities within you.

Remember, this process isn't about adding tension to your already busy life. It's about optimizing your health, making you better equipped for the challenges that life brings you – it's about inviting you to become more aware of your conditioned mind. When you sweep a dirty floor, some dust particles escape the broom, making the effort seem futile, but still, the more you sweep the cleaner it gets.

If you sincerely want this change, begin now. Do the best you can with what you have in front of you right now – with that mindset you cannot fail.

Don't focus on the end result. Let the magic happen without losing sight of what is going on in the present moment. Being too focused on the end-result (e.g. losing weight, becoming happier, etc.) will most likely bring you right back to old habits. This is a change to last a lifetime. It will affect every single aspect of your life, and it is a process that requires one small conscious step at a time.

Remember that you are worth it and that you are supported every step of the way by a higher power, the Universe, by the tools of this detox and by YOU – pick one or all of the above.

Day 1 can bring the feeling of recognizing the damage. Don't resist your own reaction to your body and try not to assign any blame or allow yourself to judge your own body based on an unrealistic popular idea of perfection — or by comparing your body to what it was five or ten years ago. Become present with the body you have right now and focus on making a sincere connection with your present state of being.

Day 1 Food & Exercise Diary

Day of the week: Saturday   **Woke up at** 8 :00

Breakfast

Time of breakfast: 8 :40

List what you eat and drink: Vegan chocolate
Shakeology with orange
essential oil.
Coffee

Lunch

Time of lunch: 12 :00

List what you eat and drink: Jimmy Johns
Country club.
Water

Dinner

Time of dinner: 8 :30

List what you eat and drink: Chinese takeout
General Tso's Chicken
House Chow Mein
Crab Rangoons (small portions)

Exercise (time, duration, type)
Walked to work + back

The Daily Love Box

Meditation (duration, place, thoughts)

After work. Home to myself. laying in bed in my dark room. How I want to succeed at this and become more positive.

Gratitude (begin your day by writing down at least 1 thing you are grateful for – actions, outcomes, experiences, people, etc.)

I am grateful for my boyfriend Izaak who is always there for me and is weathering this storm + damage right along side me.

Help (list at least 1 thing you need help with today)

I needed help with watching my son this morning until his dad came to get him.

Intentions (create 1-3 intentions or goals for the day)

Alone time. Reflection, Letting Go.

Self-care (check all that apply to your day)

Quality rest/sleep: _____

Fresh air: X

Touch/hug/massage: X

Laughter: X

Drink enough water: _____

Sunlight/daylight: X

Time alone: X

Activity/work you love: _____

Other: _____

Day 1 – Journaling.

Practice paying attention to your own personality and behavior. The best way to learn this is by closely observing your emotions, your reactions, your thoughts and the patterns of your mind. By becoming aware of your habits, you will be able to develop the instincts to make better choices. You will be able to notice thoughts and triggers that lead toward destructive emotions and behavior. Becoming aware of the habits we act out that bind, restrict and falsify our lives, we'll eventually step out of the role of prisoner to such behavior.

List at least 3 (or more) restricting and recurring beliefs that you have about your diet/food/ability to be healthy (For example: I blame my mother for the way that I eat; I don't have the will power to change; etc).

I most often tell myself I don't have the time/energy to be healthy when in reality I'm not taking/making that time for myself.

I also convince myself it's too much work + effort and I like myself alright so, I may as well just maintain my current lifestyle.
Which is not the truth because I am often disgusted and disapointed with myself and feeling like my body doesn't match the image in my mind I have for myself.

Lastly, I concern myself too much with others around me and how they want "real food" and not "health food" and I like people pleasing as well as the feeling of nurturing with my cooking.

But, if I'm not truly taking care of me and my needs I'm not fit to be taking care of others.

Day 2 – Awareness.

Mantra of the Day: "My awareness is the key that unlocks the wisdom of my body."

It may feel as if you have a long way to go until you experience any sort of 'progress,' but know that since you made the decision to do this detox, you have already changed. Your challenge is to keep it going.

Finding motivation can be tough sometimes, but it is always possible. "The gratification of a desire is in the constitution of the creature that feels it," said Ralph Waldo Emerson. In other words, where there's a will, there's a way. Especially when this will is life's highest quest: *finding a way back to you.*

When you commit to honoring your deepest desire and rediscovering your true self, no matter what, the Universe will deliver. Don't just think big deliveries, leaps and bounds, but also in sprinkles and hints. No sincere effort you make will be done in vain.

Consider what mental obstacles are holding you back: a bad mood, a negative attitude, blame or shame, a past experience, the inability to forgive yourself or others, unsupportive or self-defeating thoughts, anger, disillusion, lack of motivation, fear of the future, old attachments, delusional body shapes and/or rejecting who you are right now as a result of your negative habits, etc.

All these forms of resistance have been stored in your body and your muscles at the deepest, cellular level. In order to release them, you must become aware of their presence in your life and acknowledge them sincerely.

By allowing yourself to become aware of what is actually happening in your mind and body, you may find yourself already letting go of your discomfort. This inner awareness is potent and it may feel as if you are opening a 'can of worms', as it will bring to light other unconscious habits. Don't worry. Each layer will reveal itself at a pace that you can handle.

This practice, if consistent, has the power to blossom and grow into a deep inner transformation.

REMEMBER: YOUR DIET IS NOT YOUR BEST FRIEND, YOUR LOVER OR THERE TO FILL YOUR VOIDS. IT'S A REFLECTION OF HOW YOU FEEL ABOUT YOURSELF. DIG DEEPER.

Day 2 Food & Exercise Diary

Day of the week: Sunday   **Woke up at** 7:57

Breakfast

Time of breakfast: 8:45

List what you eat and drink: Vegan Chocolate Shakeology
with tropical fruit + orange
essential oil.

Lunch

Time of lunch: 1:00

List what you eat and drink: Salad with romaine,
avocado, tuna, cheese, olives +
ranch

Dinner

Time of dinner: 7:30

List what you eat and drink: Turkey salisbury steak
Mashed potatoes
Asparagus.

Exercise (time, duration, type)
20 min Turbo Jam 8:10 am

The Daily Love Box

Meditation (duration, place, thoughts)

My only real alone time I took today was in the car. I thought about my excuses and not doing better, I thought about how bad I want this.

Gratitude (begin your day by writing down at least 1 thing you are grateful for – actions, outcomes, experiences, people, etc.)

Grateful it's my Fri + over the next two days I can clean, plan meal, and shop to be even more successful -

Help (list at least 1 thing you need help with today)

Needed help to clear/clean the kids room to clear heater area cause its getting colder.

Intentions (create 1-3 intentions or goals for the day)

-Set the pace, wake early work out.

Self-care (check all that apply to your day)

Quality rest/sleep: ✗

Drink enough water:

Fresh air: ✗

Sunlight/daylight: ✗

Touch/hug/massage: ✗

Time alone: ✗

Laughter: ✗

Activity/work you love: ✗

Other: Good mood, reflection

Day 2 – Journaling.

List at least 3 events that have caused significant suffering in your life:

- My alcoholic parents. My abusive father. Their divorce.
- The death of John Patrick Murphy.
- Being constantly teased and bullied.
- The break up of me + my 1st love Adam.
- My relationship with my Mother.
- Leaving Mike Heines.
- My split from my Husband.
- Much of my relationship with Jeremy.
- The breaking up of my family.
- Deciding to terminate a pregnancy.

Day 3 – Awareness.

Mantra of the Day: "I choose to be consistent and sincere and give this transformation my all."

Getting through the first couple of days can be new and exciting, but as you continue to work on becoming aware of your negative habits, the path may turn long and hard.

Acknowledging a negative habit or state of mind is in itself a positive and empowering act, though it may not feel that way in the process. You are becoming aware of your false self and this is not a pleasant experience. Instead of denying or ignoring the existence of unhealthy habits, observe and acknowledge their presence.

When we are sad, angry and lonely – whether we admit to it or not – we want someone to acknowledge our pain and suffering. Why not begin by acknowledging it ourselves? Sometimes that's all we have to do – acknowledge the discomfort, the trauma and all the other negativity stored in the body – and it will start to lighten. If we feed it (literally), resist it or fight it, it will remain.

"What we resist persists."

– Carl Jung

The state of resistance is what keeps holding you back. It usually shows itself like a negative inner voice telling you to give up, distracting you from what you really want to be doing.

It's a pattern of the mind that you picked up at some point in your life. If you want to break this pattern, inquire within and invite the possibility of *doing things differently.* In Albert Einstein's words, "No problem can be solved with the same consciousness that caused it."

Try not to attach yourself to what you believe are your limitations and try not to attach to outcomes, or to the hope of feeling a certain way as a result of your efforts. Let the effects of your growing awareness be what they are. Experience them with your body and notice how you feel and act when thinking about food – are you looking forward to food because you're hungry or to distract yourself from something?

Remember that deep inside you already have all the wisdom and you already know the rules. You know what is healthy and what is not, and you know that it is going to take a sincere effort. You are now in the process of recalling that intelligence. Try not to hold onto old beliefs about your diet or fads that might have worked temporarily for you in the past. Try not to cop out for a quick fix.

Practice to make every single thing you do an invitation for deeper awareness and an intention of living life the very best you possibly can.

Day 3 Food & Exercise Diary

Day of the week: Monday   **Woke up at** 9 :30

Breakfast

Time of breakfast: 10 : 00

List what you eat and drink: Coffee with creamer

Lunch

Time of lunch: 2 : 00

List what you eat and drink: 3 pieces of pizza

Dinner

Time of dinner: 7 :45

List what you eat and drink: Roasted Chicken, quinoa, + salad.

Exercise (time, duration, type)

Deep cleaned and decluttered the huse all day.

The Daily Love Box

Meditation (duration, place, thoughts)

Late in the evening in my cozy clean home, every one in bed. How even without fully committing I already see changes.

Gratitude (begin your day by writing down at least 1 thing you are grateful for – actions, outcomes, experiences, people, etc.)

Grateful for my little home and my little life I've built. And for sharing it almost effortlessly + very enjoyably with bear.

Help (list at least 1 thing you need help with today)

Praise.
For doing a good job.

Intentions (create 1-3 intentions or goals for the day)

-clean
-Declutter
-organize

Self-care (check all that apply to your day)

Quality rest/sleep: X   Drink enough water:

Fresh air: X   Sunlight/daylight:

Touch/hug/massage: X   Time alone: X

Laughter: X   Activity/work you love: X

Other: Sense of peace. less irritability.

Day 3 – Journaling.

Describe yourself in at least 2 ways (in one word or several sentences). First, describe yourself when you are not self-accepting (e.g. I'm fat, I'm undesirable, I'm not good at my job). Then, describe yourself when you are self-accepting (e.g. I am generous, I am a good friend, I am patient).

I am too sensitive.
I take things too personally.
I'm loud.
Annoying.
I am selfish.
I overreact.
I take thing the wrong way.
I care too much of others
opinions of me.
I'm a challenge.
A burden.
An inconvienence.
I'm stubborn.

I'm caring.
Giving.
I'm loving.
I'm personable.
I'm funny.
Delightful.
I sparkle.
I'm fun to be around.
I feel.
I'm pretty.
I love deeply.
I express myself.
I'm spontaneous.
I'm a good cook.
I enjoy caring for others.
I'm a good person.

Day 4 – Awareness.

Mantra of the Day: "I am not attached to the good or bad opinions other people have about me. This is my journey and I have decided to follow it regardless of others' approval."

When you step onto the path of health and wellness, you may become aware of the unhealthy habits of the people around you. You will most likely realize that you are practicing and experiencing something different than the majority of people around you. This path can be lonely at times, but know that you are doing what is truly best for *you.*

Keep going and don't let anyone or anything stand in your way. Perhaps sooner or later, your motivation to change will inspire others to do the same. You are in this for the long run. *Learn to hold your ground.*

Tips for dealing with temptation:

1. Know that the moment of temptation will pass. It won't last forever.
2. It is possible to say "no thanks" and not miss out.
3. If the people around you aren't supportive, leave. ~~Boundaries~~
4. Don't try to justify or defend yourself. Become your message. Lead by example and the change will follow naturally.
5. If there are certain foods or habits that you have a hard time resisting, and your motivation to change isn't enough to sustain your will power, try to help yourself by making it harder for you to have access to these foods or engage in these habits. *For instance, if you have a habit of snacking late at night, don't buy any snacks and brush your teeth right after dinner. This won't make your desire go away – at least not for the first few days – but it will make it more complicated for you to go back to your old ways during moments of weakness.*
6. Be sure to hydrate yourself. Drink plenty of water, fresh juices and herbal tea.
7. Distract yourself with something – a creative activity or a physical exercise.
8. What do you really want? Ask yourself this question when you reach for that not-so-healthy comfort food. We are not attached to food per se, but to what food does to us. It connects us with feelings that we've erroneously associated with comfort food. So before hitting that snack, pause for a second, and ask yourself what feeling or sensation you're trying to satisfy. You will often be surprised by the answer. *A craving for sweets may be an indication that you need human touch – a hug or just a moment of shared mutual love and appreciation with another person.*

Go deeper every day. Keep advancing and challenge yourself. Tap into the teacher within.

Day 4 Food & Exercise Diary

Day of the week: Tuesday   **Woke up at** 9 : 30

Breakfast

Time of breakfast: 10 : 00

List what you eat and drink: 1 slice leftover pizza
coffee, water.

Lunch

Time of lunch: 12 : 30

List what you eat and drink: leftover turkey
salisbury steak and mashed
potatoes.

Dinner

Time of dinner: 7 : 45

List what you eat and drink: Turkey burgers
with homemade french fries

Exercise (time, duration, type)

Yoga 20 mins.
Before bed stretching.

The Daily Love Box

Meditation (duration, place, thoughts)

While silently snuggling Izaak
to sleep on the couch thinking
how far I've come at managing my
emotions.

Gratitude (begin your day by writing down at least 1 thing you are grateful for – actions, outcomes, experiences, people, etc.)

I am grateful for my best
friend Meg though, I haven't
been the best friend myself.

Help (list at least 1 thing you need help with today)

Help prepping and preparing
dinner.

Intentions (create 1-3 intentions or goals for the day)

- Clean the bathroom
- Do yoga
- Spend time with my friend

Self-care (check all that apply to your day)

Quality rest/sleep: ☒   Drink enough water: _____

Fresh air: ☒   Sunlight/daylight: _____

Touch/hug/massage: ☒   Time alone: ☒

Laughter: ☒   Activity/work you love: ☒

Other: Time with friends

Day 4 – Journaling.

What emotional states, moods, people and situations tempt you the most to resort to unhealthy food choices, to restrict or to binge? List all of them:

o Social situations make me want to smoke and drink which lead to more poor food choices.

o Holidays and party's with lots of tempting food choices tempt me.

o occassions dining out with friends where they say "I do it so I do too."

o Basically any time there's pizza involved.

o I restrict when I'm really focused on a goal or have set a time line for myself.

o where people are making healthy choices and I feel I should too.

Day 5 – Awareness.

Mantra of the Day: "I am conscious and awake. I resist nothing but embrace everything that happens to me and I use it to help me create my life."

There is light at the end of the tunnel. Keep going. Recognize that the path of breaking negative habits is not easy, but has great rewards along the way. Try to become present in both the easy and the hard times. It is the natural flow of life. Embrace it and surrender to it all as well as you can.

Try not to impose change to your life with force or negativity. Observe your thought patterns when dealing with temptation, lack of motivation and resistance. Instead of cussing yourself to get off the couch, let go of negativity in as much as you can, soften around it and, if able, replace it with support. Take a few deep breaths, observe the discomfort, and know that you have the ability to let it go. Allowing yourself to become an observer toward negative patterns and touch emotions can invite a more positive experience than arguing with the mind over and over again in your head.

Using forceful tactics on ourselves is just as bad as someone else using force to make us do something. The effort starts to look bigger and the benefits become harder to reap. Notice the resistance without fighting it. Be gentle and loving, but vigilant and consistent.

Try to learn from everything. The whole of life is your raw material to work with. See the strength in your weakness and how you can use it to your benefit. This is what it means to be fully present and responsible for yourself (and consequently, for others).

Think of everything that happens to you as life asking you questions. Choose each answer deliberately and with conscience.

This is not an exam. There is no right or wrong answer. There are only *present* or *distracted* answers.

Take responsibility for the actions resulting from your choices. Own who you are and embrace the consequences. It will keep you from assigning blame to others, and it will empower you, as well as alleviate unnecessary tension and anger. Why not show up 100% in life? Why not be 100% present? You are worth it.

Day 5 Food & Exercise Diary

Day of the week: Wednesday   **Woke up at** 7 : 20

Breakfast

Time of breakfast: 8 :45

List what you eat and drink: Shake

Lunch

Time of lunch: 12 : 15

List what you eat and drink: leftover chow mein

Dinner

Time of dinner: 6 :40

List what you eat and drink: Home made chicken
noodle soup
          Home made pizza pockets.

Exercise (time, duration, type)

          Stretching in the am.

The Daily Love Box

Meditation (duration, place, thoughts)

_____

_____

_____

Gratitude (begin your day by writing down at least 1 thing you are grateful for – actions, outcomes, experiences, people, etc.)

_____

_____

_____

Help (list at least 1 thing you need help with today)

_____

_____

_____

Intentions (create 1-3 intentions or goals for the day)

_____

_____

_____

Self-care (check all that apply to your day)

Quality rest/sleep: _____   Drink enough water: _____

Fresh air: _____   Sunlight/daylight: _____

Touch/hug/massage: _____   Time alone: _____

Laughter: _____   Activity/work you love: _____

Other: _____

Day 5 – Journaling.

Are you aware of even the subtlest of tendencies to force yourself to feel or attain something? Describe the elements in your life that make you feel free and, on the contrary, describe the aspects of your life where you feel constricted and imprisoned.

Day 6 – Awareness.

Mantra of the Day: "I fully accept and embrace myself. I am capable, I know enough, I am enough and I care enough about myself to make this change."

Positive self-affirmations. Positive self-affirmations. Positive self-affirmations. Your self-destruction begins in the mind. Become aware of it.

Who are you when times get tough? Who are you when effort is being asked of you? Are you supportive and nurturing toward yourself or are you violent, forceful and negative? Do you run away from your issues? Do you try to escape your life as it is?

When you feel as if you are failing, what is your inner dialogue with yourself? Are you aware of it? Do you build yourself up or do you talk yourself down?

Knowing oneself means becoming aware of the patterns of the mind. When we allow ourselves to actually listen to the dialogue of the mind, and not just feel the intensity of it in our bodies, we begin to learn how we are currently dealing with life. It may come as a surprise just how down on ourselves we are.

What does this have to do with food? Everything. If you treat yourself badly, chances are you feed yourself badly as well. Remember you are what you eat and what you have on the inside will show on the outside.

Are you a friend to yourself or an enemy? Listen and observe. If you don't like the script, change it. Acknowledge your critical inner voice and ask it to soften. In time, you will realize your own potential.

Day 6 Food & Exercise Diary

Day of the week: Monday   **Woke up at** 9 :ish

Breakfast

Time of breakfast: 9 :30

List what you eat and drink: − V choco. Shake w/ (R)
1 banana (P)

Lunch

Time of lunch: 1 :00

List what you eat and drink: − Turkey (R) Taco
Salad (G) with tomatoes, peppers +
Mush (G), Olives (O), Cheese (h)

Dinner

Time of dinner: 6 :30

List what you eat and drink: Crockpot Beef (2R)
broccoli (G) over brown rice
2 (y) + Roasted spicey
cauliflower (G)

Exercise (time, duration, type)

8pm, Total Cardio Fix 30 min

The Daily Love Box

Meditation (duration, place, thoughts)

Gratitude (begin your day by writing down at least 1 thing you are grateful for – actions, outcomes, experiences, people, etc.)

I am thankful for being able to experience the joy of the Christmas season through the eyes of my children.

Help (list at least 1 thing you need help with today)

- Help getting my work out going.

Intentions (create 1-3 intentions or goals for the day)

- Eat healthy ✓
- Drink plenty of water ✓
- Work out

Self-care (check all that apply to your day)

Quality rest/sleep: ✗   Drink enough water: ✗

Fresh air: ✗   Sunlight/daylight: ✗

Touch/hug/massage: ✗   Time alone: ✗

Laughter: ✗   Activity/work you love: ✗

Other:

Day 6 – Journaling.

Elaborate on 3 positive aspects about yourself.

REMEMBER, "ALL LIFE IS PRACTICE. PRACTICE IS ALL OF LIFE."

You already have everything you need to be the best and optimal you.

– I am Tenacious!

Nothing ever keeps me down long. I pick myself up and move forward with a new lookout and attitude.

– I am Creative

I love to get artsy. Come up with fun ideas and act silly.

– I am Caring

I love being able to do things for those around me and bring joy to others lives.

Day 7 – Awareness.

Mantra of the Day: "Am I taking life too seriously?... Be quiet, mind. You don't know what you're talking about."

Try not to overthink anything — try not to get lost in the experiences of the past or in the worries of the future.

From multiple sources, we know that in order to break a negative habit and acquire a more positive life-affirming one, we need to practice the new "replacement" habit at least 500 times or for thirty days straight, the approximate minimum time required for our neural connexions to form and strengthen new pathways in our brain.

But don't let your mind use the element of time to scare you away. Thirty days is thirty days, and if you sincerely want to, this can be a transformation that keeps unfolding for the rest of your life – not because you're following the elements of this detox, but because it is awakening wisdom within you.

The mind is extremely creative in all its ways of distraction. Giving into unhealthy habits often seems like the easier path, but deep down, maintaining unhealthy habits takes a toll that is much more severe and drags out over a much longer time than the effort it takes to set yourself free of them.

Keep taking small steps and making deeply nourishing choices that take you where you are already headed. Watch your pace and observe your thoughts.

If the anticipation of results is seeping in, acknowledge the progress you've already made and the transformation that has been taking place. Notice and recognize any feelings of self-doubt. Remember, you aren't going for perfection but a sincere connection.

You can't always do, say or be what you think is right. You aren't always going to feel confident, but you can always be you. Authenticity is what remains when all our masks are removed. It's our natural state of existence.

It is okay to feel good, to feel proud of who you are, but it is just as okay to fall and have to get back up again.

Day 7 Food & Exercise Diary

Day of the week: Tuesday   Woke up at 10 :00

Breakfast

Time of breakfast: 10 :30

List what you eat and drink: 1 hard boiled egg.
Tropical Strawberry Shake
1 Banana   tea + water

Lunch   Snack: roasted Chickpeas.

Time of lunch: 2 :00

List what you eat and drink: Tuna salad with
Veggie greek yogurt in romaine
lettuce w/ cheddar   tea +
water

Dinner

Time of dinner: 9 :00

List what you eat and drink: Spicy chicken tacos
in corn tortillas w/ cilantro, red onion,
black beans + olives
- Snack - Kale chips, Apple slices tea
+ water

Exercise (time, duration, type)
8:30 - Upper Fix 30 mins
weights + upper body.

The Daily Love Box

Meditation (duration, place, thoughts)

20 mins with tension oil.

My room. In bed in the dark.

How I need to stop taking things so personally. More positive self talk

Gratitude (begin your day by writing down at least 1 thing you are grateful for – actions, outcomes, experiences, people, etc.)

Wake up to see "Good job on Day 1 Baby!" on the dry erase calender

Very thankful for my boyfriends support.

Help (list at least 1 thing you need help with today)

- Reminding me to relax.
- Reminding me everything is not a personal attack + to not take things too personally.

Intentions (create 1-3 intentions or goals for the day)

- Fix vacuum, which I totally did!
- Clean house ✓

- Make healthy choices, workout drink water, + work on my thoughts.

Self-care (check all that apply to your day)

Quality rest/sleep: ✓   Drink enough water: ✓

Fresh air: ✓   Sunlight/daylight: ✓

Touch/hug/massage: ✓   Time alone: ✓

Laughter: ✓   Activity/work you love: ✓

Other: Good Conversation. Zack was in such a great mood tonight.

Day 7 – Journaling.

Write down 5 accomplishments that you are proud of so far, and 5 that you plan to be proud of in the future.

– Proud of being a Mommy - My son brings me so much pride.
– My weight loss transformation.
– Leaving a bad relationship.
– Making it on my own.
– Working on and learning about myself.

– Weight loss + health + emotional transformation.
– Building a healthy relationship.
– Being a good Mom.
– Continued interpersonal work + growth.
– Being successful – career, home, dreams realized.

What 3 essential qualities do you need to start developing now to help you materialize these future accomplishments?

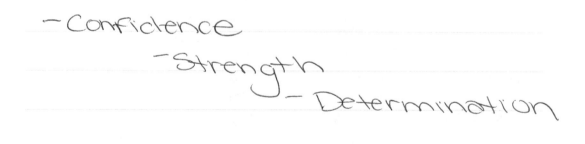

– Confidence
– Strength
– Determination

Day 8 – Awareness.

Mantra of the Day: "Thank you. Thank you. Thank you. Thank you. Thank you."

Dig deep and find the light and motivation within you. The path may seem long, but there are no lasting shortcuts. Your life is precious and so are *you*. Offer yourself and your body the best you can. If you find it hard to stay positive, try practicing gratitude.

Gratitude practice: Sit quietly every morning before your exercise routine and before breakfast and try to feel the presence of your entire body from the top of your head down to the bottom of your feet. Feel the temperature of your skin, the feeling of the clothes on your body and the foundation of the floor or the earth beneath you. Being thankful begins with acknowledging the presence of your *self*. The more you become aware of you, the more you will become aware of the support, the love and the strength around you.

Exercises for manifesting an attitude of gratitude.

Sometimes the mind, heart and body are too full of poison for you to feel grateful for them. In that case, start by recognizing the emotions, the imagery, and the opinions that hold you back from feeling grateful as well as compassionate about other people and about yourself.

What surrounds your heart? Jealousy? Anger? Blame? Shame? Guilt? Disillusion? Lack of motivation? This is *your* heart and *your* life running through it. Be honest.

Find out what's there, acknowledge its presence, and then dissolve it by accepting it and inviting it into your heart.

1. Acknowledge the presence of others – on the street, in the grocery store, at home.
2. Make eye contact with people and smile.
3. Offer a helping hand to family, friends, neighbors and co-workers. Mean it.
4. Don't be afraid to ask for help and to say "thank you."
5. Realize that your body is the greatest instrument you have to experience life. Thank it. Be grateful for it.

I SEE YOU. I RECOGNIZE YOU. I ACKNOWLEDGE YOU. THANK YOU.

Day 8 Food & Exercise Diary

Day of the week: Wednesday   **Woke up at** 6:40a

Breakfast

Time of breakfast: 7:45

List what you eat and drink: Water

T. Straw Shake() w/ Banana (R)(P)
- Hard boiled eggs (R)^2

Lunch

Time of lunch: 1:30

List what you eat and drink: Turkey (R) Taco Salad(G)
w/ onions, Cheese (B) + hot sauce.
- Snack Mushrooms + cucumber(G)
w/ Greek yogurt Dip (R)

Dinner

Time of dinner: 7:00

List what you eat and drink: Snack - Apple Slices (P)
With Cashew Butter (O).

Exercise (time, duration, type)

6:50a, Low Body 30 mins
8:30p Yoga

The Daily Love Box

Meditation (duration, place, thoughts)

This morning when I set my intentions. This evening in front of fire.

Gratitude (begin your day by writing down at least 1 thing you are grateful for – actions, outcomes, experiences, people, etc.)

- Grateful I am taking on this journey + taking care of myself.

Help (list at least 1 thing you need help with today)

- Conversation.
  Reminders.

Intentions (create 1-3 intentions or goals for the day)

- Wake early ✓
- Work out ✓
- healthy food, plenty of water.

Self-care (check all that apply to your day)

Quality rest/sleep: ✓   Drink enough water: ✓

Fresh air: ✓   Sunlight/daylight: ✓

Touch/hug/massage: ✓   Time alone: ✓

Laughter: ✓   Activity/work you love: ✓

Other:

Day 8 – Journaling.

Write down 3 material things that you are grateful for and explain why:

Write down 3 people that you are grateful and explain how they make your life better:

— My Son . He is so sweet and loving + funny and brings me such joy.
— My Mom . As a Mother I know how much she loves me + all the sacrafices raising children entails.
— Izaak. He came into my life at a rough point. Still saw me! pursued me, stays by my side. Lets me experience/ my emotions + communicates w/ me

Write down 3 situations, accomplishments or circumstances that you are grateful for and how they add to your well-being:

— I am grateful that I am a Mommy. It adds to my well being because it makes me want to be a better person.
— I am grateful for my job/ home. I worked fast and hard to make a life to support me + my son.
— I am grateful that a series of events brought Izaak into my life.

Write down 3 things, people or situations that make you feel *lucky*:

— Izaak makes me feel very lucky. The way we came together. How there for me he is. His patience + understanding

Day 9 – Awareness.

Mantra of the Day: "I am intelligent, mindful, conscious and awake. I am capable of designing my life to fit my purpose."

Autopilot: living a life of recurrent negative habits that inhibit you from feeling joy, gratitude and motivation to change. Living on autopilot prevents you from experiencing all of life's joy and beauty.

We tend to get caught up with habitual thinking – incessant regret, anger and shame of our past and incessant worry and anxiety for the future; attempts to stop habitual thinking with mind-numbing activities, such as television, gossiping and eating shuts off our mindfulness leaving us with unhealthy habits.

How do you introduce mindfulness to your life? And what does it even mean? Mindfulness is being present and conscious of what you are doing. In other words, it's observing before responding, evaluating before reacting.

Applying mindfulness to the way you choose, prepare and consume food involves presence and tapping into the deep intelligence of your body.

Mindfulness tips for when you are nourishing your body with food:

1. Try to stay present when eating. Don't watch television, talk on the phone or daydream. Be with your food and be with your body every bite of the way.
2. Let what you choose to eat be a conscious decision, not a decision based on your mood. If things aren't going your way, don't turn to food to fix it.
3. Try to stop eating when you feel the first signs of being full.
4. Practice feeling the energetic changes of the body after eating. How did the food you chose make your body feel? Energized or lethargic? Learn from your observations.

It doesn't matter what kind of background you have or what anyone else has told you about yourself. You bring something unique and special to this life, you bring *your* experience. Your conscious attitude towards yourself and your life will make all the difference.

Day 9 Food & Exercise Diary

Day of the week: Thursday   **Woke up at** 6 : 40

Breakfast

Time of breakfast: 8 : 45

List what you eat and drink: Chocolate Shake O (R)
with coffee + coconut.
egg w/ spinach, Mushroom + (G)
cheese. (B)

Lunch

Time of lunch: 12 : 30

List what you eat and drink: leftover Broccoli (G)
Beef (R) + brown rice (Y)
Snack: Apple slices (P) +
cashew butter

Dinner

Time of dinner: 6 : 00

List what you eat and drink: — Salmon (R)
With asparagus (G)
+ Yam (Y)
— Snack: Crackers (1) + Cheese (B)

Exercise (time, duration, type)
Pilates Fix 6:50am
30 mins.

The Daily Love Box

Meditation (duration, place, thoughts)

_____

_____

_____

Gratitude (begin your day by writing down at least 1 thing you are grateful for – actions, outcomes, experiences, people, etc.)

_____

_____

_____

Help (list at least 1 thing you need help with today)

_____

_____

_____

Intentions (create 1-3 intentions or goals for the day)

_____

_____

_____

Self-care (check all that apply to your day)

Quality rest/sleep: _____   Drink enough water: _____

Fresh air: _____   Sunlight/daylight: _____

Touch/hug/massage: _____   Time alone: _____

Laughter: _____   Activity/work you love: _____

Other: _____

Day 9 – Journaling.

What positive changes have you experienced in choosing, eating and preparing your food, since you started this detox, 9 days ago?

I feel more nourished
less bloated - Less guilty.
I'm really enjoying the food
I'm making + noticed I'm
craving processed food much less.

What challenges have you experienced and what are you still having a hard time letting go of?

- Emotional Roller Coaster.
- Negative Self talk + doubt.
- Highs + Lows - Feeling really pumped
+ accomplished.
    Then feeling shitty + worthless.

How do you or can you practice mindfulness in your life? Get specific about work, food and relationships. List a few ways in which you can start practicing it today:

I can practice mindfulness by slowing
        slowing down my thoughts.
down. Focusing. Paying attention.
Noticing details. Listening.
        Relaxing.
    Slowing Down

Day 10 – Awareness.

Mantra of the Day: "Burn your old ships. Build new ones. Start now. You have what it takes to be the Truest You."

Throughout our life, we have developed masks, false safe havens, particular emotions we use to hide behind or fall back on – default emotions that come back time and time again when we feel threatened and when we're under stress or challenged.

Anger, impatience, sadness and fear are the most common of these emotions. They distract us from what is actually happening and prevent us from seeing clearly. They can be all-consuming, energy draining and often tie us to other layers of negativity – guilt, shame and blame.

In times of change – especially when effort is being asked of us – our chances of discovering our own strength and manifesting any element of gratitude become drastically smaller, if we constantly entertain these negative emotions.

To deal with them, the first step is to become aware of their existence. Awareness helps you be a better observer. Being able to observe these emotions bubbling up, enables you to respond with conscience instead of simply reacting. This takes practice and you might never achieve perfection in this matter, but you will get better.

The benefits are more energy, less stress and a more positive attitude that in turn will attract other positive energies.

Nothing stays inside our bodies – this goes for emotions as well. It all comes out one way or another. We can temporarily hide our emotions with food, but what develops inside of us will eventually show on the outside – in our behavior or as illness.

Day 10 Food & Exercise Diary

Day of the week: _____   **Woke up at** _____:_____

Breakfast

Time of breakfast: _____:_____

List what you eat and drink: _____

_____

_____

Lunch

Time of lunch: _____:_____

List what you eat and drink: _____

_____

_____

Dinner

Time of dinner: _____:_____

List what you eat and drink: _____

_____

_____

Exercise (time, duration, type)

_____

_____

The Daily Love Box

Meditation (duration, place, thoughts)

_____

_____

_____

Gratitude (begin your day by writing down at least 1 thing you are grateful for – actions, outcomes, experiences, people, etc.)

_____

_____

_____

Help (list at least 1 thing you need help with today)

_____

_____

_____

Intentions (create 1-3 intentions or goals for the day)

_____

_____

_____

Self-care (check all that apply to your day)

Quality rest/sleep: _____   Drink enough water: _____

Fresh air: _____   Sunlight/daylight: _____

Touch/hug/massage: _____   Time alone: _____

Laughter: _____   Activity/work you love: _____

Other: _____

Day 10 – Journaling.

Identify your default emotion in each one of these situations:

1. How do you react when plans change at the last minute?
2. How calm are you when you are short on time?
3. How do you receive constructive feedback?
4. How do you respond to someone else's bad mood?
5. What mood are you in right before you exercise and during your exercise?

1. Depending on the plans + with who but, typically Disapointed.

2. Stressed

3. By taking it personally + feeling like a failure.

4. I too get in a bad mood

5. Tired. Self Doubting but more energized + accomplished.

"There is more wisdom in your body than in your deepest philosophy."

– Friedrich Nietzsche

FOCUS AREA II - SENSITIVITY

Key focal points:
- Developing the courage and ability to feel your body with awareness and with clarity, especially in times of stress, strong emotions and when eating.
- Growing your awareness of the energy expressed through your emotions and how it impacts the body, your intentions and the quality of your nourishment.
- Learn to recognize feelings and sensitivities in the body and connect them to your recurring actions, situations and emotions.
- Identify the foods that are both feeding and numbing your default emotions.
- Gaining a feeling for how the foods you choose to nourish your body with make you feel physically, energetically, creatively, mentally and emotionally.

Our genes have often been blamed for our predisposition to certain traits that are believed to develop in us almost against our will. But, given the appropriate nurture, not even those of us who have inherited a clear predisposition to certain negative habits or traits will end up developing any of them if these genes or predisposition are not stimulated.

In other words, despite patterns of habits that we've gained through an inherited predisposition or via other external influences, we are a process of change and we are highly influential and sensitive to *what we do*. In addition, there is a high probability that we are not who and what we think we are. We are in fact, much more.

We all have default emotions. We acquire them, mostly during our first seven years of life, when we move around as sponges soaking up the environment around us. Although we are able to learn and change throughout the rest of our lives, this can be a significant influence during our first years of human experience. Whatever we absorb during this period, whatever habits and tastes we acquire, are imprinted deep into our psyche, and can take much longer to become aware of, sensitive to and also to undo.

We eventually get to a point where our emotions become default, because they've undergone years and years of repetition. These default emotions are not final, but they can be mistaken for our real selves and can create a vicious cycle in our lives – especially when they are closely related to food. When food is used to numb and feed emotions, it assists in reinforcing them. In time, these emotions start demanding the same type of food.

Food alters and directly affects our emotions and thus our physical body. If a type of food is not feeding or resulting in constructive, life-affirming emotions, it is probably the other way around. Nothing is neutral – especially not what you put in your body.

Your emotions are a strong barometer. They communicate to you the state of your inner world, and – if rightly used – they can be powerful indicators of what is going on inside.

For the next 10 days, we'll learn to not only become aware of, but to feel the effects that our recurring habits and thought patterns have had on our ability to nourish ourselves with food. It can be scary and hard to feel the body, just as it is hard to hear your own whispers among so much unnecessary noise – internal and external – that we are bombarded with daily.

At first, you may realize that you cannot feel parts of your body. You may already have what you believe to be a clear perception of the parts of you that you don't love, have deemed unworthy, not the right shape or not good enough. You may or may not also be aware of the places within your body that hold the most tension, stress and trauma. No matter to what degree, with practice, you can become more sensitive to all parts of you and learn to function as a whole being.

Your inner voice may also be imperceptible, but once you learn its language, you'll hear it in a crowd. By learning to listen to your emotions, you'll understand – and even surprise – yourself. You'll also learn to identify what they're really asking for and how they impact you physically.

Parallel to how our recurring patterns and default emotions impact us physically is the energy we derive from food. We eat (with body and mind) only to produce more energy and to keep on living. So we must consume energy in order to survive and, in surviving, we keep on producing more energy that is passed on to our surroundings. We all feed on energy – our own and that of others. We truly are what we eat, in every possible way.

We can't deliver something different than that which we consume. The world gives, we take, we add our signature, only to give it back to the world. If we don't take what we really want and need from the world around us, we won't metabolize it optimally and we certainly won't give back to the world any more than a mediocre by-product that has little to do with us – other than keeping us alive at least for a while longer.

What we're after is not just surviving, but becoming fully and abundantly alive. Abundance, and not scarcity, is our natural human status.

Life is made of energy. Just like a thought (your mind's food) can poison your day with negative energy and, after endless and mindless repetition, be delivered back into the world through your actions – perpetuating the damage that this energy has done to you in the first place – food can pollute your magnificent, sacred body with contrary, negative energy, that will add to the existing negativity in your life and in the world.

The vicious cycle will complete itself with even more negativity. Because when mind and body are upset, we look for band-aids, cool-aids, shortcuts, quick fixes, and fast food that will not cure but only temporarily and apparently calm our madness instead of looking at the cause and, in that inner search, find the cure.

By learning how to identify the energy we consume on a daily basis, we become more sensitive to our food choices and thus, our bodies. We begin to listen to our body and heart. We re-initiate our life-long conversation with our truest selves and learn to nurture ourselves with food that provides life-giving energy (instead of life-negating, survival-mode limited energy). In other words, we become more alive. We will wake up and begin to experience clarity and focus like never before.

Feel your body.

> *"Paying attention to and staying with finer and finer sensations within the body is one of the surest ways to steady the wandering mind."*
>
> **– Ravi Rvindra**

Day 11 – Sensitivity.

Mantra of the Day: "What I resist, persists."

We are told to be kind to others. But the way we treat others is a mirror of the way we treat ourselves. Our life begins in our own heart. We can't always give what we haven't received, so we must be kind to ourselves first and foremost before anyone else. We do this by acknowledging the feelings of resistance in us. When you acknowledge resistance in any form, feel it. Allow yourself to become aware that it is there. Sometimes all it takes is acknowledging this resistance. Sometimes it takes a little more patience, introspection and work. It can take a few moments, days, years, even a lifetime, but it's your work and the path itself can lead to a deeper understanding of who you are. If you want this, allow yourself to go deeper.

When acknowledging resistance or discomfort in our bodies, we nearly always avoid it or distract ourselves from it. When you feel the resistance, become conscious of it, but also of your response to it. Never ignore your resistance or your pain and try not to treat it with pain-killers (unhealthy food or other distractions). Use pain-healers instead (see examples below).

Old habits can get extremely creative on their way out the door, but you are innately more intelligent and creative than them. The fact that you discovered emotional pain in your body isn't a justification to reward yourself with junk food. Sure you've learned that these short-term pleasures cover up the pain, but you know that it doesn't heal anything in the long run. It prolongs the struggle and postpones the healing process.

Our body is fully conscious of its own negativity, but it can't withstand it forever. The negative habits we develop are unhealthy and unconscious responses to this same resistance. Instead of really healing us, they cause additional resistance, a lack of sensitivity, and negativity adding to a vicious cycle.

When becoming aware of resistance, instead of resorting to old negative habits, try something that has a real potential to soothe your emotional pain, that is healthy and that also truly feels good. There are a lot of healthy activities and foods that will serve this purpose. Healthy is synonymous with pleasure. The most long-lasting and satisfying type of pleasure you can know.

Healthy pain-healers:
- Exercise (e.g. yoga, fitness, sports).
- Meditation.
- Helping a friend, neighbor, family-member or co-worker.
- Volunteering.
- Journaling, creative writing.
- Other artistic outlets (e.g. painting, singing, dancing).
- A walk in nature.
- Finding inspiration through museums, conversations, concerts or other life-affirming activities.

Day 11 Food & Exercise Diary

Day of the week: _____   **Woke up at** _____:_____

Breakfast

Time of breakfast: _____:_____

List what you eat and drink: _____

_____

_____

Lunch

Time of lunch: _____:_____

List what you eat and drink: _____

_____

_____

Dinner

Time of dinner: _____:_____

List what you eat and drink: _____

_____

_____

Exercise (time, duration, type)

_____

_____

The Daily Love Box

Meditation (duration, place, thoughts)

_____

_____

_____

Gratitude (begin your day by writing down at least 1 thing you are grateful for – actions, outcomes, experiences, people, etc.)

_____

_____

_____

Help (list at least 1 thing you need help with today)

_____

_____

_____

Intentions (create 1-3 intentions or goals for the day)

_____

_____

_____

Self-care (check all that apply to your day)

Quality rest/sleep: _____   Drink enough water: _____

Fresh air: _____   Sunlight/daylight: _____

Touch/hug/massage: _____   Time alone: _____

Laughter: _____   Activity/work you love: _____

Other: _____

Day 11 – Journaling.

Describe and write down at least 3 (or more) instances or areas in your life where you experience recurring resistance. Don't concern yourself about being right, assigning blame or justifying your feelings.

Exercise: Focus on each one of these areas, one at a time. Allow yourself to become sensitive to how they make you feel physically and mentally. Then, try to momentarily let go. Take a deep breath and give permission to your body to relax as best as you can. This relaxation safely allows your body (and mind) to release the resistance in layers.

Make a list of pain-healers (as described on the previous page) that could work for you – healthy activities that will not only make you feel better, but also give you pleasure.

Day 12 – Sensitivity.

Mantra of the Day: "Abandon all expectation. Let go. Receive."

When we are not in tune with ourselves, our expectations tend to be unaligned, leading us to disappointment.

Expectations can be an indicator of how much we live in the past (e.g. we might want the body of our twenty-two year old self, etc.) or fear the future. Reliving the past and being fearful of the future can add unnecessary tension to our lives (e.g. when we worry about the results of the detox and how long it's going to take to feel or see a change, etc.).

Expectations can cause the *What If* anxiety. *What if* I fail? *What if* my family thinks this or that of me? *What if* I need more time? *What if* I'm not enough? *What if* I'll never be perfect?

Ironically, when you let go of this way of thinking, you can actually receive and get more. When you admit that you are enough, that you're the best you can be right now, you are *ready to become more*.

Expectations take up a lot of space in our minds and create tension in the body. But, what do you do without them? What is the difference between expectations, goals and intentions?

> *Expectations are typically positive or negative extremes and they're often found on a superficial (irrational) level.*
>
> *Goals point to an end — a result achieved after the efforts are over with.*
>
> *Intentions are symbolic of the effort you have to put into achieving the goals — something you sit with for period of time, something you can work at in the present moment.*

Expectations add extra stress and pressure. So try to let go of them or at least soften around them. Stick to your intentions and your goals.

Try to live in the present as best as you possibly can. Understand, feel and acknowledge where you are right now – this is all you have to work with – not your younger body or your future expectations. Take a deep breath and one step at a time.

What is your reality? It's within you. Discover it. Don't be someone else's quote. Make your own – right now.

Day 12 Food & Exercise Diary

Day of the week: _____   **Woke up at** ____:____

Breakfast

Time of breakfast: ____:____

List what you eat and drink: _____

_____

_____

_____

Lunch

Time of lunch: ____:____

List what you eat and drink: _____

_____

_____

_____

Dinner

Time of dinner: ____:____

List what you eat and drink: _____

_____

_____

_____

Exercise (time, duration, type)

_____

_____

The Daily Love Box

Meditation (duration, place, thoughts)

Gratitude (begin your day by writing down at least 1 thing you are grateful for – actions, outcomes, experiences, people, etc.)

Help (list at least 1 thing you need help with today)

Intentions (create 1-3 intentions or goals for the day)

Self-care (check all that apply to your day)

Quality rest/sleep: ⎯⎯⎯⎯   Drink enough water: ⎯⎯⎯⎯

Fresh air: ⎯⎯⎯⎯   Sunlight/daylight: ⎯⎯⎯⎯

Touch/hug/massage: ⎯⎯⎯⎯   Time alone: ⎯⎯⎯⎯

Laughter: ⎯⎯⎯⎯   Activity/work you love: ⎯⎯⎯⎯

Other: ⎯⎯⎯⎯

Day 12 – Journaling.

Contemplate the words that describe your self-identity: positive, negative and neutral. Make a list of descriptive words for each of these categories. List them without shame and guilt.

After writing them down, contemplate and acknowledge how these descriptions A) make you feel and B) distract you from living in the present moment (i.e. Do they describe who you are presently, the person you were in the past or the person you want to be in the future?).

Day 13 – Sensitivity.

Mantra of the Day: "I am satisfied. I have enough. I don't need, want or try to get more."

How full does your belly have to be? When should you stop eating? If you have a habit of overeating, the warning signal arrives long after our body has actually had enough food to work with.

Aside from experiencing a desensitizing of the body, we might also use food for comfort and to calm negative emotions or reinforce addiction to our emotional rollercoaster of unhealthy extremes. Since this has nothing to do with hunger, being full won't make us stop eating. We'll keep eating until our negative emotions are good and numb or until we experience the emotional highs we are addicted to.

Today, try to eat food for your body's sake. Let your choices be about what your body needs, not what your feelings make you crave. Choose what you know to be nutritious. Add a salad to one of your meals – not just any salad, but try to find or make your ideal, nutritious salad. Find the pleasure in eating healthy food.

Practice to serve yourself the right portions. If you don't know the right portions for you, start with small ones and pay close attention to your body's signs of being full. When the signs appear, stop eating.

Set yourself free from fear and tension by only taking what you presently need. Don't eat for the future.

Day 13 Food & Exercise Diary

Day of the week: _____   **Woke up at** _____ : _____

Breakfast

Time of breakfast: _____ : _____

List what you eat and drink: _____

_____

_____

Lunch

Time of lunch: _____ : _____

List what you eat and drink: _____

_____

_____

Dinner

Time of dinner: _____ : _____

List what you eat and drink: _____

_____

_____

Exercise (time, duration, type)

_____

_____

The Daily Love Box

Meditation (duration, place, thoughts)

_____

_____

_____

Gratitude (begin your day by writing down at least 1 thing you are grateful for – actions, outcomes, experiences, people, etc.)

_____

_____

_____

Help (list at least 1 thing you need help with today)

_____

_____

_____

Intentions (create 1-3 intentions or goals for the day)

_____

_____

_____

Self-care (check all that apply to your day)

Quality rest/sleep: _____   Drink enough water: _____

Fresh air: _____   Sunlight/daylight: _____

Touch/hug/massage: _____   Time alone: _____

Laughter: _____   Activity/work you love: _____

Other: _____

Day 13 – Journaling.

Describe the feeling you get when you overeat. What are your first physical indications that you've eaten enough? If you can, identify 3 physical signals. Can you think of how you may be ignoring these signals throughout the day?

Identify 1 to 3 situations today where you could have served yourself less, where you could have said *no*, where you would have been okay with less or where you felt the signs of being full, but the familiar eating habits made you ignore it.

Day 14 – Sensitivity.

Mantra of the Day: "Life conspires with me to help me fulfill my purpose."

You are now two weeks in. When it hurts the most, that's when your internal self-healing process is really working with you, not against you, to recalibrate.

Know that when you hit these walls or tough spots, you've located the places within, where work needs to be done. These parts of you are dying for your attention.

It's easy to adopt a victim attitude, to feel that life conspires against you. Many people who practice a superficial positivity are really pessimists at heart. They have just chosen a smile as their defense mechanism. This is not something negative per se, but smiling isn't synonymous with genuine optimism or confidence.

If you remember that you've been born against great odds, that you are an unrepeatable, unique, irreplaceable human being, you might realize that instead of *against you*, life has actually been conspiring *with you* all along.

The same universe, that made you possible, is now trying to help you survive the odds and welcome you to life. For you to do so, it provides you with all kinds of unexpected, life-transforming help through your journey.

Learn how to pay attention and become sensitive to what you are experiencing in the present moment.

The perception of pain is the first and most important indication of growth. You are breaking an old system. The fortress you've inhabited is finally being demolished and it hurts, no matter how great your new building plans may be. What can you do? Stay with it. Don't give up. You are already on your way.

Day 14 Food & Exercise Diary

Day of the week: _____ **Woke up at** _____ : _____

Breakfast

Time of breakfast: _____ : _____

List what you eat and drink: _____

_____

_____

Lunch

Time of lunch: _____ : _____

List what you eat and drink: _____

_____

_____

Dinner

Time of dinner: _____ : _____

List what you eat and drink: _____

_____

_____

Exercise (time, duration, type)

_____

_____

The Daily Love Box

Meditation (duration, place, thoughts)

_____

_____

_____

Gratitude (begin your day by writing down at least 1 thing you are grateful for – actions, outcomes, experiences, people, etc.)

_____

_____

_____

Help (list at least 1 thing you need help with today)

_____

_____

_____

Intentions (create 1-3 intentions or goals for the day)

_____

_____

_____

Self-care (check all that apply to your day)

Quality rest/sleep: _____   Drink enough water: _____

Fresh air: _____   Sunlight/daylight: _____

Touch/hug/massage: _____   Time alone: _____

Laughter: _____   Activity/work you love: _____

Other: _____

Day 14 – Journaling.

Describe the pain you are currently experiencing on your detox journey. Then describe what would happen if you quit and returned to your previous habits. Describe how both options make you feel.

Day 15 – Sensitivity.

Mantra of the Day: "I am capable, diligent and persistent. I am fully equipped and powerful beyond measure. I can create and enjoy the life I imagine."

Your glass is half full. If you've fallen off track at some point on your way, today is the day to forgive yourself and get back up again. Nobody is perfect.

"Without darkness there can be no light."

– Lao Tzu

Note all your shortcomings, stare your imperfections in the face and try to find the humorous side to every defect. Take a break from yourself and laugh at your own foolishness. With seriousness comes tension, stress and unforgiving expectations.

Don't hide your ugliness, your madness, but perceive, acknowledge and feel it. By consistently practicing this, you can learn to become friends with it like a blessed monster in disguise.

Tips for finding inner space:

- Forgive others.
- Forgive yourself.
- Accept others.
- Accept yourself.
- Don't blame.
- Don't attach yourself to descriptive words of your perceived self-identity no matter how positive or negative they are.
- Laugh more.
- Let go of things and people that no longer serve you in the most nourishing way.
- Limit or completely stop watching violent television shows and movies.
- Remove any negative talk about yourself from your life.
- Remove negative talk about others.

If you can embrace a frame of mind that everything is happening for the best possible reason, you'll be able to invite life in. Having an open mind creates a lot of space within our minds as it cuts out excessive worry and fear.

Try to welcome every experience no matter how challenging they seem. This will liberate you from carrying around unnecessary baggage by alleviating stress and fear. It will also keep you present.

Ask every bout of negativity to dance. Invite it into your arms and into your heart. Don't fight it, resist it or attempt to banish it. Just invite it in. You can give it what it needs – *your attention* – and feel it as clearly as you can in the present moment.

Day 15 Food & Exercise Diary

Day of the week: _____   **Woke up at** _____ : _____

Breakfast

Time of breakfast: _____ : _____

List what you eat and drink: _____

_____

_____

_____

Lunch

Time of lunch: _____ : _____

List what you eat and drink: _____

_____

_____

_____

Dinner

Time of dinner: _____ : _____

List what you eat and drink: _____

_____

_____

_____

Exercise (time, duration, type)

_____

_____

_____

The Daily Love Box

Meditation (duration, place, thoughts)

_____

_____

_____

Gratitude (begin your day by writing down at least 1 thing you are grateful for – actions, outcomes, experiences, people, etc.)

_____

_____

_____

Help (list at least 1 thing you need help with today)

_____

_____

_____

Intentions (create 1-3 intentions or goals for the day)

_____

_____

_____

Self-care (check all that apply to your day)

Quality rest/sleep: _____   Drink enough water: _____

Fresh air: _____   Sunlight/daylight: _____

Touch/hug/massage: _____   Time alone: _____

Laughter: _____   Activity/work you love: _____

Other: _____

Day 15 – Journaling.

Write down at least 3 aspects of yourself that you dislike. They can be both physical and mental. Write down these shortcomings, read them out loud and acknowledge how they make you feel.

Write down at least 3 aspects of yourself that you like. They can be both physical and mental. Write down these shortcomings, read them out loud and acknowledge how they make you feel.

When you are finished writing, try to let go of both lists. Invite the possibility that no matter how positive or negative these words are, you are much more than you think – you are more than you can imagine. You are limitless and have the potential to tap into a deeper wisdom, beyond good or bad, beautiful or ugly, right or wrong.

Day 16 – Sensitivity.

Mantra of the Day: "I care about others deeply, but I don't depend on their opinions. I must follow my journey at all costs."

Look around you. Learn to observe the people you come into contact with daily. What are they saying when they're not saying anything out loud? What are your expectations when it comes to them? How does it feel to be around them and how does their presence in your life make you feel?

Understand that people will only give you what they have. They can't give you any more or any less at any given time, and you can't change that. Whatever support, or lack thereof, you get from them is not a reflection of you, but of them.

So instead of demanding something that is not there, learn to listen to their song. Just like you are now becoming more aware and sensitive of your needs, you will become more aware and sensitive to the needs of others – especially the people you love and share your life with. In most cases, you'll be amazed to discover how most of them are also trapped in a story that is not theirs. Their inability to be supportive can actually be their own cry for help in disguise.

In other words: save your own life. Don't wait or expect anyone else to do it for you. Take care of you, first and foremost.

Notice when you start competing with or judge others and try to identify your real feelings behind this. If the need to compare yourself to others comes from a place of envy, fear or anger, know that it all comes back to you, which essentially means that it's not important *how* you compare to others. The only person you are really competing with is yourself.

Let go of false beliefs of perfection and unrealistic expectations concerning what others should do, be and look like, but more importantly, do this for yourself. Allow and invite yourself to keep transforming into who *you* truly are.

If you're feeling alone on this path, know that you are not. If you were, you wouldn't be reading this right now. When you are ready and when you really want to, you'll connect with others on the same path.

Remember, just because you are on a journey of truth and self-discovery, it doesn't make you right and others wrong. As your awareness and sensitivity grows, be sure to allow your compassion and motivation to go deeper. Stay level minded. Lead by example and with compassion. You have what it takes.

Day 16 Food & Exercise Diary

Day of the week: _____   **Woke up at** _____:_____

Breakfast

Time of breakfast: _____:_____

List what you eat and drink: _____

_____

_____

Lunch

Time of lunch: _____:_____

List what you eat and drink: _____

_____

_____

Dinner

Time of dinner: _____:_____

List what you eat and drink: _____

_____

_____

Exercise (time, duration, type)

_____

_____

The Daily Love Box

Meditation (duration, place, thoughts)

_____

_____

_____

Gratitude (begin your day by writing down at least 1 thing you are grateful for –
actions, outcomes, experiences, people, etc.)

_____

_____

_____

Help (list at least 1 thing you need help with today)

_____

_____

_____

Intentions (create 1-3 intentions or goals for the day)

_____

_____

_____

Self-care (check all that apply to your day)

Quality rest/sleep: _____   Drink enough water: _____

Fresh air: _____   Sunlight/daylight: _____

Touch/hug/massage: _____   Time alone: _____

Laughter: _____   Activity/work you love: _____

Other: _____

Day 16 – Journaling.

How important is it to you to get the approval of others? How do you react when you don't get their attention when you demand/or feel you need it? List at least 3 (or more) alternative exercises you can practice instead of getting upset, angry or frustrated with that person.

Have you noticed even the slightest tendency to judge others based on this detox awareness and sensitivity building? Describe how you have felt and list at least 3 (or more) points of view you can adopt versus becoming judgmental and/or righteous.

Day 17 – Sensitivity.

Mantra of the Day: "I am. I am. I am. I am."

Try not to control or force your body into feeling things. Try letting these changes come as naturally as you can. You are not trying to label yourself with a new sensitivity, but to discover that which you already possess. It's a process of reawakening and rediscovery.

Remember, all the treasures you're looking for are already yours. You are now inviting the possibility of discovering them. When trying to find something that you don't posses naturally, all kinds of factors may get in your way. But this is not the case. That's why you cannot fail, because the treasures already belong to you. Yet, as much as you posses them, life is still short. It is your choice to start making use of what you have, live it abundantly and to enjoy it.

When you invite the possibility of living in the present moment, feeling your body clearly and consciously, time will take on an entire new meaning.

The mind is creatively twisted in coming up with distractions, false stories, fantasies, finding excuses and assigning blame. Another way of doing this, as discussed in previous sections, is by labeling you with descriptive words. How many of the excuses you have used to avoid making an effort, relate to how you define yourself? Your age, your type of person, your experience, your past – all based on stereotypical profiles created and repeated by others.

Try to explore the space behind your descriptive words, masks and labels. Question how you do things. Challenge your labels. Explore what feels best to you. Keep seeking what your heart sings for – the stuff that makes you want to live and share it with others.

Follow the trail. Follow life's clues leading back to you. Redefine *You* with you.

Day 17 Food & Exercise Diary

Day of the week: _____   **Woke up at** _____ : _____

Breakfast

Time of breakfast: _____ : _____

List what you eat and drink: _____

_____

_____

Lunch

Time of lunch: _____ : _____

List what you eat and drink: _____

_____

_____

Dinner

Time of dinner: _____ : _____

List what you eat and drink: _____

_____

_____

Exercise (time, duration, type)

_____

_____

The Daily Love Box

Meditation (duration, place, thoughts)

_____

_____

_____

Gratitude (begin your day by writing down at least 1 thing you are grateful for – actions, outcomes, experiences, people, etc.)

_____

_____

_____

Help (list at least 1 thing you need help with today)

_____

_____

_____

Intentions (create 1-3 intentions or goals for the day)

_____

_____

_____

Self-care (check all that apply to your day)

Quality rest/sleep: _____   Drink enough water: _____

Fresh air: _____   Sunlight/daylight: _____

Touch/hug/massage: _____   Time alone: _____

Laughter: _____   Activity/work you love: _____

Other: _____

Day 17 – Journaling.

How are you truly feeling, mentally and physically? In a few paragraphs, describe what is going through your body and mind, as if you were talking to a good old friend and you had all the space and safety you need to truly open up.

Be careful not to fill in the blanks with mindless chatter, default feelings and falsified sensations. Let the blanks speak to you. And if they don't, remain a blank space for a little while longer.

Day 18 – Sensitivity.

Mantra of the Day: "I feel my pain. I also feel the pain of others and regard them with the same compassion, for they are also faced with a great battle."

When you feel somebody's pain, a lot of things that you didn't previously understand can begin to make sense. Most people – yourself included – don't act the way they want to, but the way their story tells them to. And if they are strangers to their own heart and body, and their story runs on default emotions – from scripts written and imposed by others – they can't help but spread that to others.

Hurt people hurt people.

Breathe in this truth and forgive yourself. Sit with your mistakes and look them in the eye. You didn't know any better. Even if some part of you did, you weren't aware or ready to act on it. Let it go.

This is your time. Right now.

Know that all the pain that you've hidden and locked up inside your body, didn't fit well going in, despite the deceiving, yet soothing, emotion that you felt when you locked it up. It will naturally hurt as it comes out. But the more you try to hold on to it, the longer it will define you and the harder it will be to let it go.

You don't need to analyze the past in order to let it go. Just start to loosen the grip. Trust your body. It knows exactly what to do. Follow its lead.

Breathe.

Things, people and sources of energy that it might be time to let go of:
- Negative attitudes.
- Self-defeating thoughts.
- Fear, guilt, anxiety, anger, envy.
- Failures and trauma of the past.
- Worries about the future.
- Unnecessary material items, clothes, furniture, etc.
- Toxic relationships.
- Limiting labels about you identity, personality and being.

Day 18 Food & Exercise Diary

Day of the week: _____   **Woke up at** _____ : _____

Breakfast

Time of breakfast: _____ : _____

List what you eat and drink: _____

_____

_____

_____

Lunch

Time of lunch: _____ : _____

List what you eat and drink: _____

_____

_____

_____

Dinner

Time of dinner: _____ : _____

List what you eat and drink: _____

_____

_____

_____

Exercise (time, duration, type)

_____

_____

The Daily Love Box

Meditation (duration, place, thoughts)

_____

_____

_____

Gratitude (begin your day by writing down at least 1 thing you are grateful for – actions, outcomes, experiences, people, etc.)

_____

_____

_____

Help (list at least 1 thing you need help with today)

_____

_____

_____

Intentions (create 1-3 intentions or goals for the day)

_____

_____

_____

Self-care (check all that apply to your day)

Quality rest/sleep: _____   Drink enough water: _____

Fresh air: _____   Sunlight/daylight: _____

Touch/hug/massage: _____   Time alone: _____

Laughter: _____   Activity/work you love: _____

Other: _____

Day 18 – Journaling.

The best way to let go of your demons is by facing them – things that are still locked up in the basement of your heart, causing you unwanted (and unnecessary) default pain.

As for your body, have you been ignoring any physical pain or discomfort? Think twice before you answer. Re-examine your body. Many people live with so much extra pain that they consider *normal*. Sometimes they are even inadvertently punishing themselves for unforgiven issues of the past.

But physical pain or discomfort is neither normal, nor should it serve as a punishment, and there is always a way out. Pain can be our best ally if used correctly. Use it as a signal – as an indication that some-thing inside is not right. Your task is to dig up that something.

What pain do you need to be more aware of? What have you not forgiven yourself for?

Day 19 – Sensitivity.

Mantra of the day: "I commit to being truthful and honest with myself and others, above all things."

Telling the truth is not limited to the greater issues in your life. It goes beyond that and into your skin and bones – it is energy, it translates into feeling and it can contribute to the state of our bodies significantly. Truth demands your attention and enough courage to face life without lying to yourself about your story.

Truth is not an affirmation or a phase, it is a state of being, and it holds a place in our bodies.

Truth is a relationship of pure, raw honesty with your innermost self. Only when you are truthful and honest can you really see and feel yourself for who you are (equally beautiful and terrifying). And only when you start seeing and feeling yourself, can you understand your own motives and finally forgive yourself (and others). Authentic, healthy self-love demands brutal, raw honesty.

Through the day, try to pay attention not just to the greater, obvious lies in your life (if any) but also to the smaller, unnoticed ones – the ones lying at the root of your modus operandi, the ones that really dictate the discourse on which you live your life. When found, try to connect with how they make you feel.

Be honest with what you put into your body, your mouth, your ears and your mind and be honest with what comes out of you... and, become aware and sensitive to the reactions of your body.

- *Instead of making an excuse the next time someone asks you to do something that you don't want to do, be honest and politely decline.*
- *When choosing something unhealthy, acknowledge the justification whole-heartedly.*
- *When skipping your daily exercise, fess up to yourself and acknowledge whether the excuse was truthful or not.*

Say what you mean and mean what you say, and explore if this creates more freedom and space in your body and in your life. Lies lead to strings and webs that are difficult to keep track of, and they create mountains of stress, guilt and worry.

Keep it simple, keep it real and keep it honest. We'll dive deeper into Honesty in the remaining 10 days.

Day 19 Food & Exercise Diary

Day of the week: ....   **Woke up at** .... : ....

Breakfast

Time of breakfast: .... : ....

List what you eat and drink: ....

....

....

....

Lunch

Time of lunch: .... : ....

List what you eat and drink: ....

....

....

....

Dinner

Time of dinner: .... : ....

List what you eat and drink: ....

....

....

....

Exercise (time, duration, type)

....

....

The Daily Love Box

Meditation (duration, place, thoughts)

_____

_____

_____

Gratitude (begin your day by writing down at least 1 thing you are grateful for – actions, outcomes, experiences, people, etc.)

_____

_____

_____

Help (list at least 1 thing you need help with today)

_____

_____

_____

Intentions (create 1-3 intentions or goals for the day)

_____

_____

_____

Self-care (check all that apply to your day)

Quality rest/sleep: _____   Drink enough water: _____

Fresh air: _____   Sunlight/daylight: _____

Touch/hug/massage: _____   Time alone: _____

Laughter: _____   Activity/work you love: _____

Other: _____

Day 19 – Journaling.

List 3 (or more) lies you have been feeding yourself or have told others recently. List them and then describe how they've made you feel both physically and mentally.

When you experience these emotions, what inner affirmation brings them out? The affirmation is usually the lie, but it can be buried deep inside, so put on your self-examination glasses and look closely.

nsitivity.

"I deserve the best of what life has to offer. I deserve to be happy, loved and fulfilled. A beautiful life is my birthright."

If you're even slightly uncomfortable with this mantra, you should repeat it (out loud if possible) until you believe it.

If you practice becoming aware and sensitive toward your choices, actions and reactions to life you will eventually grow beyond any false beliefs about yourself.

Your innermost beliefs create the emotions that fuel your food choices, which feed your body with energy. If you have limited energy to work with, your body will have limited options in what it can do with it, and because making changes requires energy, it's easy to be caught up in a negative circle of unhealthy choices and low energy.

Inescapable?

Once you even get an inkling of these unhealthy habits, you are no longer on autopilot – just like the moment you bring your focus out of the incessant dialogue of the mind and place it on your breath – you are no longer lost.

Today, think about how you reward yourself. We all do, or life would be unbearable. We feel that we deserve a 'break' or a 'reward' or a 'day off' every now and then – and we do. But why do we choose the opposite of a break or a reward or a day off to actually "reward" ourselves? A large pizza, a bottle of alcohol, an unnecessary lie or a fight with a loved one...

A *reward* should actually be a reward – something that invites you to feel authentically calm, empowered, healthy and alive, recharge your batteries, give you rest, restore you, fulfill you, add to your well-being, make your life easier – not something that just looks like a reward and cause even further damage on the inside.

Here is a list of healthy rewards:

- A nap.
- A walk in nature.
- A rejuvenating bath.
- A massage.
- A healthy snack.
- An inspiring activity.
- A class you've always wanted to take.
- A weekend getaway in a healthy, natural and nourishing environment.
- A few hours in the company of someone you love.

Reward yourself with life-affirming, you-affirming nourishment.

Day 20 Food & Exercise Diary

Day of the week: _____   **Woke up at** _____ : _____

Breakfast

Time of breakfast: _____ : _____

List what you eat and drink: _____

_____

_____

_____

Lunch

Time of lunch: _____ : _____

List what you eat and drink: _____

_____

_____

_____

Dinner

Time of dinner: _____ : _____

List what you eat and drink: _____

_____

_____

_____

Exercise (time, duration, type)

_____

_____

The Daily Love Box

Meditation (duration, place, thoughts)

_____

_____

_____

Gratitude (begin your day by writing down at least 1 thing you are grateful for – actions, outcomes, experiences, people, etc.)

_____

_____

_____

Help (list at least 1 thing you need help with today)

_____

_____

_____

Intentions (create 1-3 intentions or goals for the day)

_____

_____

_____

Self-care (check all that apply to your day)

Quality rest/sleep: _____   Drink enough water: _____

Fresh air: _____   Sunlight/daylight: _____

Touch/hug/massage: _____   Time alone: _____

Laughter: _____   Activity/work you love: _____

Other: _____

Day 20 – Journaling.

What rewards in disguise can you identify in your daily choices? This is most noticeable in your food but it is present in every area of your life.

List at least 3 (or more) food (and/or other) choices that pose as rewards but have nothing restoring or rewarding about them, other than momentarily or apparently calming you down. Describe how they make you feel, physically and mentally.

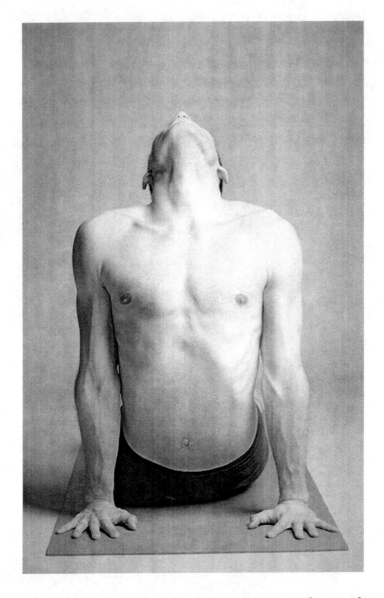

"The most fundamental aggression to ourselves, the most fundamental harm we can do to ourselves, is to remain ignorant by not having the courage and the respect to look at ourselves honestly and gently."

— Pema Chödrön

FOCUS AREA III - HONESTY

Key focal points:
- Learning how to uncover and identify deceitful patterns that pose as truth.
- Learning to practice raw honesty with yourself (and others) by embracing truth as a modus operandi, not dependent on feelings, emotions or moods.
- Learning to become aware and sensitive to the intentions and motivations we have behind thoughts, words, interactions, reactions and choices.
- Learning to perceive truthfully without control or force (mental and physical).
- Exploring the possibility of no longer associating ourselves with preconceived descriptive words that define and limit our self-image.
- Discovering what food choices align with your innermost truth and can be embraced with full honesty, love and respect for yourself.

Honesty: your mirror; the degree in which you are able to face, understand and live your life to its fullest; the gateway to your real self and the chance to live abundantly.

Honesty is not a feeling but the way you face and respond to your emotions and everything else in your life. It's a modus operandi, one we have been taught to ignore and neglect. But it is, indeed, a *lifetime* practice. No authentic change is possible if not made form a place of honesty within your self. Honesty gets you to the center. It cleanses your heart of all the lying toxins and it liberates you. Not only does truthfulness set you free, it creates more space in your heart, mind and body. It eliminates unnecessary tension and stress by softening the incessant chatter of the mind. When you embody the truth, when you live with truth in your life, you create an enormous amount of balance. This balance does not carry with it baggage – anger/shame/regret/disillusion about the past – nor does it engage in worries or anxiety of the future, not even of death.

There is a primordial and ultimate power in truth – power to act in accordance with what you really need and deeply want without giving in to stories that are not your own. There is also courage. Truth strips you naked of all your excuses, hiding places, excessive, unnecessary life padding, and throws you into the unknown, so you can design your own reality – honesty *is* reality. It leaves you only the option of living your life to its fullest. Truth demands creative responsibility for your life. The more you practice truthfulness to yourself and your purpose, the more your life, freedom and creativity will expand. For the next 10 days, we'll be practicing truth and honesty with ourselves. We'll re-examine our choices, separated from the grip of our emotions.

You may not be a doctor, a nutritional counselor or a health expert, but no one knows more about your body or what is best for it than you. You must save your own life. No one else can.

Day 21 – Honesty.

Mantra of the Day: "I have the ability to admit my mistakes. I have the courage to take responsibility for my actions. I am my will."

The mind can be our best friend and our worst enemy. It can play tricks on us and talk us out of our decisions or strengthen us and talk us into a truthful practice. Its versatility is what makes it extraordinary.

As long as we remember that we are more than what we think and that, just like our body the mind can serve as a life-saver or as a life-sucker; we can begin to use our mind's extraordinary abilities to create the life we want, rather than let it trick us into one we don't.

But first, we must identify the garbage. Through the day, start taking out the trash, literally and figuratively. Identify what choices are not serving you. Practice radical honesty in doing so. No safety tricks. There is no safe place other than your own truth. Declare your truths. *You* truly know what is good for you and what isn't.

Choose what does the least harm and the best good.

When you speak the truth you also offer others the chance to do the same. When we speak and hear the truth, it resonates with us. It invites a deep connection and a feeling of comfort and ease. Truth creates space and alleviates unnecessary chatter and worry.

The mind is always in motion, thinking, remembering, shouting and whispering in a constant pursuit of truth – but notice that when it hears the truth and connects with it, its dialogue ceases if only for a few moments. It rests.

When we speak or hear others speak untruthfully, it feels uncomfortable and invokes stress, even at very subtle levels. It may even create incessant thoughts and worry.

Become as mindful as you can of your truths. Connect with their energetic force in your body.

Day 21 Food & Exercise Diary

Day of the week: _____   **Woke up at** _____ : _____

Breakfast

Time of breakfast: _____ : _____

List what you eat and drink: _____

_____

_____

_____

Lunch

Time of lunch: _____ : _____

List what you eat and drink: _____

_____

_____

_____

Dinner

Time of dinner: _____ : _____

List what you eat and drink: _____

_____

_____

_____

Exercise (time, duration, type)

_____

_____

The Daily Love Box

Meditation (duration, place, thoughts)

_____

_____

_____

Gratitude (begin your day by writing down at least 1 thing you are grateful for – actions, outcomes, experiences, people, etc.)

_____

_____

_____

Help (list at least 1 thing you need help with today)

_____

_____

_____

Intentions (create 1-3 intentions or goals for the day)

_____

_____

_____

Self-care (check all that apply to your day)

Quality rest/sleep: _____   Drink enough water: _____

Fresh air: _____   Sunlight/daylight: _____

Touch/hug/massage: _____   Time alone: _____

Laughter: _____   Activity/work you love: _____

Other: _____

Day 21 – Journaling.

List a few (or more) food and mental items that you are attached to but are not truly serving you. Allow yourself to be brutally honest. Then, list what would happen if you let go of them.

What mental and physical benefits would you experience if you let go? What would the downside be? Describe your day without engaging in any of these practices. What would you choose instead?

Day 22 – Honesty.

Mantra of the Day: "I am resourceful and manifold. I can learn from any situation. Everything and everyone has something to teach me. Nothing is in vain."

All good things in life come slow: food, real friends, great accomplishments, authentic change, genuine joy and transformation, new habits, true love... how we relate to ourselves and the rest of the world. Most of us have been born and nurtured in a fast society, where value is placed on efficiency rather than effectiveness – quantity versus quality.

But life is not a get-it-over-with driving examination. What we need is not to be efficient at it and pass through the obstacles as quickly as we can. There is no license awarded at the end. Our life is our license to live it.

Instead, we must be effective, unfold our life to its fullest and greatest degree, live up to the mission and response this life is asking from us.

In this greater scenario, each situation, detail and person has something to teach us and something good will come out of all things yet. So be patient with your growth. Try to find the joy in everything. It's a process of gaining and letting go, gaining and letting go. Keep on asking the difficult questions. Look around you and notice the beauty and lessons present even in the perceivably least appealing things, people or situations.

"When the student is ready, the teacher appears."

– Unknown

As your awareness and sensitivity grows and as you invite truthfulness into your journey, life can become clear. As the fog starts to slowly disappear, see and feel everything as clearly as you can. Regard every experience as an invitation to get to know your self on a deeper level. All signs lead back to you.

Day 22 Food & Exercise Diary

Day of the week: _____   **Woke up at** _____ : _____

Breakfast

Time of breakfast: _____ : _____

List what you eat and drink: _____

_____

_____

_____

Lunch

Time of lunch: _____ : _____

List what you eat and drink: _____

_____

_____

_____

Dinner

Time of dinner: _____ : _____

List what you eat and drink: _____

_____

_____

_____

Exercise (time, duration, type)

_____

_____

The Daily Love Box

Meditation (duration, place, thoughts)

_____

_____

_____

Gratitude (begin your day by writing down at least 1 thing you are grateful for – actions, outcomes, experiences, people, etc.)

_____

_____

_____

Help (list at least 1 thing you need help with today)

_____

_____

_____

Intentions (create 1-3 intentions or goals for the day)

_____

_____

_____

Self-care (check all that apply to your day)

Quality rest/sleep: _____   Drink enough water: _____

Fresh air: _____   Sunlight/daylight: _____

Touch/hug/massage: _____   Time alone: _____

Laughter: _____   Activity/work you love: _____

Other: _____

Day 22 – Journaling.

List a few of the little white lies, or the polite lies you've told lately. List some ways in which you could have handled each situation differently.

Telling polite lies is something most of us do on a habitual, even unconscious basis — these white lies can lead to a lot of mistrust not only toward other people, but also toward ourselves.

Take a deep breath. Sit on a different side of things for a while longer and invite a new understanding in.

Day 23 – Honesty.

Mantra of the Day: "My mind is a temple. I ventilate it every morning and clean it every night. I choose my thoughts wisely. Life whispers to me all the time. I have an inner compass to guide me."

What is your mind's daily talk? It is estimated that 80% of our thoughts are the same as the day before. What patterns do you walk daily, and which of them amount to your fulfillment, or to your further estrangement from yourself? Is your inner talk destructive or constructive? Or a little bit of both?

If you're not sure, be careful. We are surrounded by destructive patterns on all levels of our social interaction. And every human pattern and feeling is contagious. You must build yourself a safe, healthy home inside, from where you can face the world.

Your mind is the only place where you are fully allowed, the only house to which you have keys. If you don't use them, someone else will occupy it. You must go inside, clean it thoroughly and decorate it according to what you *really* want. It's not just your right, it is your duty, as a creative organism.

Focus on your inner talk today. What are you really saying to yourself on a daily basis? What's your tone, what are the truths (or lies) you repeat like daily, subconscious mantras?

Day 23 Food & Exercise Diary

Day of the week: _____   **Woke up at** ____ : _____

Breakfast

Time of breakfast: _____ : _____

List what you eat and drink: _____

_____

_____

Lunch

Time of lunch: _____ : _____

List what you eat and drink: _____

_____

_____

Dinner

Time of dinner: _____ : _____

List what you eat and drink: _____

_____

_____

Exercise (time, duration, type)

_____

_____

The Daily Love Box

Meditation (duration, place, thoughts)

_____

_____

_____

Gratitude (begin your day by writing down at least 1 thing you are grateful for – actions, outcomes, experiences, people, etc.)

_____

_____

_____

Help (list at least 1 thing you need help with today)

_____

_____

_____

Intentions (create 1-3 intentions or goals for the day)

_____

_____

_____

Self-care (check all that apply to your day)

Quality rest/sleep: _____   Drink enough water: _____

Fresh air: _____   Sunlight/daylight: _____

Touch/hug/massage: _____   Time alone: _____

Laughter: _____   Activity/work you love: _____

Other: _____

Day 23 – Journaling.

What are any significant lies you have told in your lifetime that you'd like to confess to? List as many as you'd like.

Do you have the courage to make amends right now? Explain why or why not. Be honest with your justifications, excuses and with assigning any blame.

Whether or not you physically make amends, how does the thought of making such amends make you feel?

Day 24 – Honesty.

Mantra of the Day: "I refuse to excuse myself from living my purpose. I also refuse to apologize for being my true badass self. I am who I choose to be and I must do all that I can to embody my own, unique truth."

There are two big detours on the way back to You. One is making excuses for living up to your purpose and the other is, apologizing when you *do* live up to it.

The excuses come first. They are a way of avoiding your purpose, and they pull you back and off track. They may come by the way of distractions or even deeper, almost imperceptible mind tricks.

Today, try to identify your excuses – from the teensy weensy to the most obvious.

How does your Self excuse you from realizing it? How do you cheat yourself out of living and get dragged on survival mode? Stare your excuses in the face, it's the only way to confront them and kick them out of your system.

Next, let's hit the apologies. When you start living with no excuses, as soon as your newly found freedom feels threatened, you tend to apologize for being you. Stop that. Don't ever apologize for being honest and true to yourself, no matter how uncomfortable this may make others.

Truth can piss people off, but it also sets them free. When you quit the excuses, your adventure begins, and only a genuinely lived adventure can inspire others to create and live theirs. Apologizing for your freedom will give your excuses more power to pull you back and cut it short.

Note: Apologizing may come under the form of an invisible hand, pulling you back from expressing your full self, your true wonder – even after you've already started living it. It may also come under the form of false modesty, but really, it's just another mask. Take it off. Own your greatness.

Day 24 Food & Exercise Diary

Day of the week: _____   **Woke up at** _____:_____

Breakfast

Time of breakfast: _____:_____

List what you eat and drink: _____

_____

_____

_____

Lunch

Time of lunch: _____:_____

List what you eat and drink: _____

_____

_____

_____

Dinner

Time of dinner: _____:_____

List what you eat and drink: _____

_____

_____

_____

Exercise (time, duration, type)

_____

_____

The Daily Love Box

Meditation (duration, place, thoughts)

_____

_____

_____

Gratitude (begin your day by writing down at least 1 thing you are grateful for – actions, outcomes, experiences, people, etc.)

_____

_____

_____

Help (list at least 1 thing you need help with today)

_____

_____

_____

Intentions (create 1-3 intentions or goals for the day)

_____

_____

_____

Self-care (check all that apply to your day)

Quality rest/sleep: _____   Drink enough water: _____

Fresh air: _____   Sunlight/daylight: _____

Touch/hug/massage: _____   Time alone: _____

Laughter: _____   Activity/work you love: _____

Other: _____

Day 24 – Journaling.

Identify at least 3 (or more) excuses in your daily doings (at least one of these excuses should be related to your food choices) that keep you from being yourself.

Identify three situations or scenarios in which, for fear, lack of self-belief and insecurity, you might be indirectly apologizing about your convictions and truths.

Day 25 – Honesty.

Mantra of the Day: "I am making progress. I am blessed. I am alive and moving. Slowly, but steadily, I advance in the direction of my dreams."

Today, take the time to just be and allow truth to bring you back into the alignment of reality.

Go for a walk, practice your craft, create your art, spend time with a friend, laugh, hug, kiss, love someone, an animal, a tree... Do something that makes you genuinely and truthfully happy to be alive – not a substitute for pain that will end up bringing you more of what you don't want, but an activity that heals pain by recycling it into a healthier, creative option to appreciate life.

However, taking the time to just be doesn't have to mean engaging in any particular activity. It also doesn't mean taking the time to incessantly talk. Allowing your self to 'be' is mainly about being in the moment as fully and presently as possible. Allow yourself to sit in the spaciousness of truth without trying to create a falsified situation, outcome or result.

Taking time to just be recharges your batteries and helps you assess your progress. Do something that makes you feel good. Life is short and made of moments. Don't wait until you have it all figured out to create a safe oasis where you can recharge and get ready for the next phase of your journey.

Mark the time for a 'Date with Self' on your calendar. Be vigilant about keeping it to yourself. Take comfort in the time you prepare for yourself.

Day 25 Food & Exercise Diary

Day of the week: _____   **Woke up at** ____ : ____

Breakfast

Time of breakfast: ____ : ____

List what you eat and drink: _____

_____

_____

_____

Lunch

Time of lunch: ____ : ____

List what you eat and drink: _____

_____

_____

_____

Dinner

Time of dinner: ____ : ____

List what you eat and drink: _____

_____

_____

_____

Exercise (time, duration, type)

_____

_____

The Daily Love Box

Meditation (duration, place, thoughts)

_____

_____

_____

Gratitude (begin your day by writing down at least 1 thing you are grateful for – actions, outcomes, experiences, people, etc.)

_____

_____

_____

Help (list at least 1 thing you need help with today)

_____

_____

_____

Intentions (create 1-3 intentions or goals for the day)

_____

_____

_____

Self-care (check all that apply to your day)

Quality rest/sleep: _____   Drink enough water: _____

Fresh air: _____   Sunlight/daylight: _____

Touch/hug/massage: _____   Time alone: _____

Laughter: _____   Activity/work you love: _____

Other: _____

Day 25 – Journaling.

Make a list of 21 activities that truly give you pleasure and make life more enjoyable. Let it be truthful, realistic and approachable. Let this be your list and not a replica of someone else's.

Happiness is a journey and it is made up of little things. Don't let you life pass you by in a rush. Stop and smell these flowers. Put this list on your fridge and try to do at least one of these things every day, for the next three weeks.

Day 26 – Honesty.

Mantra of the Day: "I am my own, unique, personal version of life. I sing to my own tune. I have a Universe inside me. I am life, force, creativity and abundance. This life is my collage. I am actively engaged and committed to creating it to the best of my ability."

Even if we are all made of the same energy and material, we are each unique combinations of truth. You have your own story to write and share with the world, both like and unlike anybody else's.

The similarities between us help us feel less alone and inspire us to continue. The differences point out our individuality and uniqueness. When you start facing your life, love manifests itself both ways, painting a full, multi-dimensional picture.

You can't be similar to anyone unless you're also different and you can't fully appreciate the difference, unless you also sense the similarity. One needs the other.

By being honest with your truth, and honoring your goals – which in turn, lead to your mission and purpose – you will also be honest with others, supporting and inspiring them to honor theirs.

Your originality goes hand in hand with that of others. When you are 'yourself' you automatically invite others to become themselves.

Awake from your slumber. You are the artist and your life is the masterpiece.

Day 26 Food & Exercise Diary

Day of the week: _____   **Woke up at** ____ : ____

Breakfast

Time of breakfast: ____ : ____

List what you eat and drink: _____

_____

_____

Lunch

Time of lunch: ____ : ____

List what you eat and drink: _____

_____

_____

Dinner

Time of dinner: ____ : ____

List what you eat and drink: _____

_____

_____

Exercise (time, duration, type)

_____

_____

The Daily Love Box

Meditation (duration, place, thoughts)

_____

_____

_____

Gratitude (begin your day by writing down at least 1 thing you are grateful for – actions, outcomes, experiences, people, etc.)

_____

_____

_____

Help (list at least 1 thing you need help with today)

_____

_____

_____

Intentions (create 1-3 intentions or goals for the day)

_____

_____

_____

Self-care (check all that apply to your day)

Quality rest/sleep: _____   Drink enough water: _____

Fresh air: _____   Sunlight/daylight: _____

Touch/hug/massage: _____   Time alone: _____

Laughter: _____   Activity/work you love: _____

Other: _____

Day 26 – Journaling.

What is your truth? What are your truths? Stand truthfully right now in your own being. Conceal nothing. Write a 10-point personal manifesto of what you stand for. Write it in present tense, as if you are already living by these principles, because merely by writing them down, you're on your way.

Day 27 – Honesty.

Mantra of the Day: "I will never leave my body, and no one knows my body better than me. I commit to honoring it, protecting it and turning it into my home for the rest of my days."

You are not a number, a statistic or a medical record. You are a living wonder, a verb, the beautiful synergy of thousands of simultaneous reactions, occurring as we speak. You are not fixed in any way. You can be transformed, for you are not a unit, you are a process.

Your body contains the answers to your deepest questions. You are on your way back to you. You already encapsulate the cure for all your pain and sickness. All you have to do is keep discovering it.

It is true that there are many paths that lead toward self-realization – their common denominator: the climb. We all have to make an effort to get there. But we must not fool ourselves with the notion of what effort really means. There is a clear difference between effort that takes but never gives back and effort that offers something back on a deeper level.

A lot of times we give up because we believe the effort is too great. We misconstrue the reality of the impact of our current effort to remain exactly where we are.

Yes, there are certainly an extraordinary amount of tools out there, but one of the most effective, one that we need, in order to remain alive, is sustenance.

As you transform your words, your thoughts and your life towards a more honest approach, allow your food and nourishment choices to align accordingly. You know more about your body and what is best for you than any other person or theory.

Day 27 Food & Exercise Diary

Day of the week: _____   **Woke up at** _____ : _____

Breakfast

Time of breakfast: _____ : _____

List what you eat and drink: _____

_____

_____

Lunch

Time of lunch: _____ : _____

List what you eat and drink: _____

_____

_____

Dinner

Time of dinner: _____ : _____

List what you eat and drink: _____

_____

_____

Exercise (time, duration, type)

_____

_____

The Daily Love Box

Meditation (duration, place, thoughts)

_____

_____

_____

Gratitude (begin your day by writing down at least 1 thing you are grateful for – actions, outcomes, experiences, people, etc.)

_____

_____

_____

Help (list at least 1 thing you need help with today)

_____

_____

_____

Intentions (create 1-3 intentions or goals for the day)

_____

_____

_____

Self-care (check all that apply to your day)

Quality rest/sleep: _____   Drink enough water: _____

Fresh air: _____   Sunlight/daylight: _____

Touch/hug/massage: _____   Time alone: _____

Laughter: _____   Activity/work you love: _____

Other: _____

Day 27 – Journaling.

Commit to truthfulness. Be honest with what you put into your body and what you allow to come out of it. Truth is a genuine teacher.

List at least 3 (or more) obstacles you perceive to be holding you back from eating, choosing, living, acting and/or speaking truthfully. For each obstacle listed, describe how realistic the obstacle actually is and if you have caught yourself making excuses, assigning blame or even creating a polite lie.

Day 28 – Honesty.

Mantra of the Day: "Truth is in every heart. It is my essence and my birthright."

Your life is composed of layers. Your symphony will not harmonize until all your layers are nurtured. It all starts with your Foundation: Learn your *Why* and your *Who*. It continues with your Connection: Learn your *How* and with *Whom*. And it unfolds with your Expression: Learn and practice your *What*.

Every idea, if persisted on, will eventually manifest, acquire a "body." You become what you consistently do. And you do what you consistently think of. Your daily thoughts will be built upon a foundation of basic beliefs defining your core and outlook on life. Examine and inquire how real your beliefs are and if they are even your own.

Your *What* is the most visible part of you, your upper layer. It is your creation or set of creations. It can be anything from the sparkle in your eye, career, a family, a business, a work of art or any other activities in which your life manifests. The deepest layer, your *Why*, is encapsulated in and expressed through your *What*.

Through today, try to think of your layers and identify them. The clearer you get about each one, the easier it will be to nurture them and help yourself grow in the direction you really want your life to go.

Day 28 Food & Exercise Diary

Day of the week: _____   **Woke up at** _____ : _____

Breakfast

Time of breakfast: _____ : _____

List what you eat and drink: _____

_____

_____

_____

Lunch

Time of lunch: _____ : _____

List what you eat and drink: _____

_____

_____

_____

Dinner

Time of dinner: _____ : _____

List what you eat and drink: _____

_____

_____

_____

Exercise (time, duration, type)

_____

_____

The Daily Love Box

Meditation (duration, place, thoughts)

Gratitude (begin your day by writing down at least 1 thing you are grateful for – actions, outcomes, experiences, people, etc.)

Help (list at least 1 thing you need help with today)

Intentions (create 1-3 intentions or goals for the day)

Self-care (check all that apply to your day)

Quality rest/sleep: _____

Drink enough water: _____

Fresh air: _____

Sunlight/daylight: _____

Touch/hug/massage: _____

Time alone: _____

Laughter: _____

Activity/work you love: _____

Other: _____

Day 28 – Journaling.

Identify your Foundation, your Connection and your Expression:

- *Foundation — Why & Who.*
- *Connection — How & Whom.*
- *Expression — What.*

Allow your ability as an alchemist to turn your dreams into reality by connecting to what is truthful.

The whole is greater than the sum of its parts and life is a symphony depending on individual sounds from an entire orchestra of instruments. But before music can be made, each instrument needs to be tuned.

Day 29 – Honesty.

Mantra of the Day: "I am the way, the truth and the life. I am the key and door to Me."

Knowing the talk and walking the talk are two very different things. And we, twenty-first century creatures love to talk. But what are your feet saying? What is your revolution and how are you walking it? What are you doing each day as a natural extension of your talk?

Although all change must start inside, actions are a good way to measure our growth and identify what works and what may still be holding us back. Just like feelings are a barometer of our deepest self, actions are our materialized energy. They are our physical extension in this world and they seal off and carry out what our innermost desires, beliefs and expectations dictate.

If our revolution begins in the heart, our evolution can only be understood and appreciated through our facts. By paying close attention to our actions, we learn to identify the cause beyond the tricks of the mind and our true motivation.

Access your ability and power to speak and live from inspiration — allow yourself to be motivated by a deeper truth that is not only factual, but that illuminates, that can be shared and received and that reflects a deeper state of reality.

Meditate on your actions today, as they are louder than words to the world around you. Let them speak and face the truth contained in them. And if what you observe does not match the truth you want to live by, go back inside and re-examine your core beliefs and the possible obstacles that may come in the way of these beliefs materializing into equivalent actions.

Day 29 Food & Exercise Diary

Day of the week: _____   **Woke up at** _____ : _____

Breakfast

Time of breakfast: _____ : _____

List what you eat and drink: _____

_____

_____

_____

Lunch

Time of lunch: _____ : _____

List what you eat and drink: _____

_____

_____

_____

Dinner

Time of dinner: _____ : _____

List what you eat and drink: _____

_____

_____

_____

Exercise (time, duration, type)

_____

_____

The Daily Love Box

Meditation (duration, place, thoughts)

Gratitude (begin your day by writing down at least 1 thing you are grateful for – actions, outcomes, experiences, people, etc.)

Help (list at least 1 thing you need help with today)

Intentions (create 1-3 intentions or goals for the day)

Self-care (check all that apply to your day)

Quality rest/sleep: _____   Drink enough water: _____

Fresh air: _____   Sunlight/daylight: _____

Touch/hug/massage: _____   Time alone: _____

Laughter: _____   Activity/work you love: _____

Other: _____

Day 29 – Journaling.

Write out your mission. Not your business mission, your family's mission, your ought-to mission but your own mission. Your Life's Mission. It should include every area in your life – physical, mental, spiritual, emotional, relationships, work and any other life project – and intend to carry out your unique message, your call, into the world.

It's not just about what you want. It's about how what you want fits in this world, at this point in history, and how it will affect you and others. Your life begins with you, but as you evolve through it, *you* become vast and your work and influence expands. Keep these elements in mind when drafting your life's mission.

Draft it out, cut what doesn't work, edit, rewrite. Nothing is final and your mission may change or be readapted as time passes. This is only meant to help you have a clearer vision of it, at any given moment.

Carry it with you, in your purse, wallet, on your screen. Memorize it until it turns into a natural extension of your talk.

Day 30 – Honesty.

Mantra of the Day: "I am a creative individual in the flow of change, capable of not just surviving but equipped to live life abundantly, serenely and joyfully aware."

Welcome to the first day of the rest of your life. You've made it. Hug yourself today. Throw a party in your honor. You deserve every bit of joy this life can offer you. You deserve to be loved, cared for, believed in, understood and accepted. This is your time. These truths are your birthright. Claim them now and don't settle for anything less.

Breathe in the beauty around you and make it yours. The world is your canvas. Life is conspiring with you (not against you). The Universe will deliver when you call. Design the rest of your life based on this reassurance.

There is no finality, no destination, just the continuous, creative discovery of your beautiful, worthy and unique self. The end is the means and the means is the end. You put one step in front of the other, one breath after another, day after day after day.

There is no past or future, no beginning or end. Our perception of time is just a way of organizing our life. In essence, there is only Now. You are here now. That's all that matters.

You are a composition, a work of art. Let your self-creation work its wonders on you... through the invitation of continuous awareness, sensitivity and radical honesty.

Day 30 Food & Exercise Diary

Day of the week: _____   **Woke up at** _____ : _____

Breakfast

Time of breakfast: _____ : _____

List what you eat and drink: _____

_____

_____

_____

Lunch

Time of lunch: _____ : _____

List what you eat and drink: _____

_____

_____

_____

Dinner

Time of dinner: _____ : _____

List what you eat and drink: _____

_____

_____

_____

Exercise (time, duration, type)

_____

_____

The Daily Love Box

Meditation (duration, place, thoughts)

_____

_____

_____

Gratitude (begin your day by writing down at least 1 thing you are grateful for – actions, outcomes, experiences, people, etc.)

_____

_____

_____

Help (list at least 1 thing you need help with today)

_____

_____

_____

Intentions (create 1-3 intentions or goals for the day)

_____

_____

_____

Self-care (check all that apply to your day)

Quality rest/sleep: _____   Drink enough water: _____

Fresh air: _____   Sunlight/daylight: _____

Touch/hug/massage: _____   Time alone: _____

Laughter: _____   Activity/work you love: _____

Other: _____

Day 30 – Journaling.

Write your present self a letter from the future you.

Ten years have passed from today. What would the 10-year older *you* say to your current you? Where are you 10 years from now? Who is with you? What have you accomplished? What are your feelings about your life and how has your vision of the world and action field expanded over a decade?

Include all your dreams – big and small. Leave nothing out. Play will help your imagination unfold. And imagination is your creative engine. Learn to use it to drive forward your desires.

Knowing your destination makes all the difference because it will soon transform into your journey. And even though change is to be expected, learning and practicing your purpose will also help you recognize change, and readapt your script to honor your constant evolving and becoming.

Welcome to the Rest of Your Life.

Life is short. How much time do we have?

For centuries, we have been conditioned to find superficial meaning and depend on our outer circumstances for our well-being, sense of purpose and personal happiness — most of which have been reliant on education, the status we've achieved or how big our wallet is.

Instead of acting (taking individual, conscious creative action), we've been wired to react to the influences of the greedy, the fearful flock, those with the power to repress and, as a result, we have all inevitably generated more of the same. We ceaselessly disengage the power of the individual self's connection with the collected consciousness for a continual separation of wholeness of not only ourselves, but to others and all life forms.

For most of our life, we've misunderstood our purpose. We aren't really here to find ourselves, as we are not lost. We are here to see, feel, acknowledge and create our whole selves to the best of our ability. And the good news is that we already come equipped with everything we need in order to be the people we already hold inside.

Healing doesn't turn us into different people. Healing unveils our own truths and our real selves – the truths we've ignored since the world was made, the ones we've kept in hiding for fear that they might be too great to be true, and powerful beyond any rigid regime. The frantic side of our egos and self-imposed limitations have been holding us hostage in the basement of our soul. And it's not easy to get out.

Change requires unprecedented action. Change is not comfortable. Because it rebels against the stagnant, it questions the norm and all the habits, beliefs and values that keep you from returning to You.

When you've been living in a dark room all your life and you suddenly turn on the light, your eyes will hurt. Not because they don't want or desperately need the light, but because they've forgotten what light is for or how to use it. You were made to prevail through the darkness and move forward into the light. The darkness is a mere function of the process of light and both are used to create the world through images – but there must be an acknowledgment of both for a more sound truth to exist.

Every new creation begins with a subtle or significant destruction. Without any kind of death, there would be no resurrection to the truest version of your self. If you don't shed your old skin and let go of what no longer serves you, there is no space for the new.

You have the ability to stand firm through this growing pain, this shedding of layers. You can conquer your fear of being great, of seeing your true self face to face, in all your magnificence. You can survive the birth pain of letting this self out.

Surrender to this higher love, this higher form, this higher self and let the universe express itself through you. Trust beyond the surface level. Go deeper. Give yourself permission to see, feel and become aware of who and what you are, if only for a small moment at a time. And keep going.

You're not alone. We're 99% you. Every one of us is a representation of something greater than ourselves, a shared universal consciousness that we each embody to the best of our ability. We are deeply and inextricably connected beyond our wildest imagination. And the only way we can access the fountain of life is by going inside — through inner inquiry, openness to the subconscious and an observation of consciousness.

We each have a direct line with the source of all our power, creativity and aliveness, through our own heart. There is no salvation outside of you. Any revelation that leads to real change must start inside. Any external revolution must first be a revolution of the self. Any significant discovery must begin as a continuous self-discovery. There is no other way to access truth than through your own doors of perception and personal experience.

Nothing good can come from the outside unless it has first been sown inside your own chest. Everything in your life is a personal recognition. All the people you meet, your DNA, all of your experiences – good and bad and everything in between – are open doors inviting you into your inner world, where defeat or victory are no longer important but where exists a well of your own personal wisdom, self-acceptance, connection and all-embracing love.

This is why no one can save you – because no one can do a better job at You than You. No one can access the source of life available to you, other than You.

Change starts with simple choices. The outcome of your life is reduced to small decisions you make every day, every hour and even every minute. And it is fuelled by the belief that you are powerful beyond measure and that these choices can alter the course of your entire existence.

So start somewhere. Start with one of the most significant, basic aspects of your life – your nourishment – and start choosing your food and your thoughts wisely. For this is the stuff life is made of and you will soon become the outer version of your inner daily choices. They might be small, but they are shaping the course of your destiny.

Start nourishing yourself everyday like you're your best friend, your best ally, your doctor, your guru, the master of your fate. Love yourself like your life depended on it. Because it does.

It is out of this love that all your inner greatness will find the strength and courage to come alive, and it is out of the ordinary, little steps you take every day that the extraordinary will be built.

This is Your Life.

Accept it. Love it. Use it.

And give it away.

The Beginning...

About the authors

Tanya Markul

Co-Creator of RebelleWellness.com and Co-Founder / Editor in Chief at RebelleSociety.com. She holds a Bachelor of Science in Journalism and a Master's Degree in Business. She is now a full-time devoted student of yoga, meditation and creative wellness alchemy. In 2009 she became a certified yoga teacher. She has been practicing and studying with master teachers from all over the world exploring and becoming deeply inspired by different traditions of yoga. She believes there is no greater classroom than life in this body and the freedom of the present moment. She also believes life is a practice of discovery of individual nourishment, healing, self-acceptance and the most authentic creative expression of the self. What are you waiting for? Connect with her on Facebook & Twitter @tanyamarkul or via email: tanya@rebellewellness.com.

Andréa Balt

Co-Creator of RebelleWellness.com and Co-Founder / Editor in Chief at RebelleSociety.com. She holds a Bachelor of Arts in Journalism & Mass Communication, an MFA in Creative Writing and a Health Coach degree from the Institute for Integrative Nutrition®. She practices a holistic reintegration of Art & Wellness and, through her work, she aims to reflect the wholeness of the human experience, leading to a personal awakening and an inevitable Creative Renaissance. She is also trying to reinstate Creativity as one of our essential Human Rights. Learn more about her work at AndreaBalt.com, and connect with her on Facebook & Twitter @andreabalt, Instagram @creativerehab or via email: andrea@rebellewellness.com.

THANK YOU!

We are immensely grateful for the chance to come together and create this wellness guidebook to personal alchemy, self-recovery and awakening. We'd like to express our deepest gratitude and appreciation to the people who've helped, inspired and supported us on this journey.

Christian Ryd Hoegsberg – For your endless patience, unshakeable sturdiness and strength, elite editing talents, business-oriented superpowers, strategic consulting and publishing support.

Jessica Durivage Kerridge – For all your encouragement and contribution throughout the creation of this project, your contagious joy and enthusiasm, wisdom, flexibility and open-mindedness. And for lending your wonderful *Where is My Guru* radio space to our Wellness Alchemy.

Our team behind the scenes of Rebelle Society – For your hard, excellent and impeccable work, for believing in us and our mission, for loving what is and for being present, helpful and kind. Not to mention your leadership, your astounding heart-felt communication and your creative roots.

To nature, this planet, our teachers, mentors, masters, friends, family and all life forms – For seeing, planting and nurturing these universal truths in us, for supporting and understanding us even when we made it difficult, for loving us for what we are, and for constantly reminding us of the ultimate Alchemy: the ability to transform ourselves and recreate our lives from the inside out, right here and right now.

The 30-Day Wellness Alchemist Detox is
a production of RebelleWellness.com

Connect with us on
Facebook, Twitter & Instagram:
@RebelleWellness

Or email us:
info@rebellewellness.com

If you enjoyed this guidebook and it has been a useful companion on your 30-day journey back to you, give us a shout-out on Social Media and let us know:

Mention it through a status update, or post a selfie reading it, on Facebook, Twitter and Instagram. Make sure you tag us – @RebelleWellness on each of these platforms so we can connect with you. Use the hashtag #wellnessalchemy.

If you know anyone whose life might be touched or changed by this book, pay it forward and gift them a copy. Inspiration is the first step to authentic and long-lasting change.

CPSIA information can be obtained at www.ICGtesting.com
Printed in the USA
BVOW01s1410191014

371137BV00018B/441/P